I0459596

Body Language - Bye-Bye Bluffer

Quickly Master the Skills of Reading People, Winning Them Over Effortlessly, and Closing Deals with Confidence!

A.M. Corby

Clover Pinnacle Publishing

Body Language: Bye-Bye Bluffer

Copyright © 2024 by A.M. Corby

All rights reserved.

Clover Pinnacle Publishing, LLC

No portion of this book may be reproduced, in any form or by any means, graphic, elec-
tronic, or mechanical, including photocopying, recording, taping, any informational
storage and retrieval systems, any manner whatsoever without written permission
from the publisher or author, except in any case of brief passages embodied in critical
articles and reviews.

Under no circumstances will any blame or legal responsibility be held against the publisher, or author, for any damages, reparation, or monetary loss due to the information
contained within this book. Either directly or indirectly. You are responsible for your
own choices, actions, and results.

Legal Notice:

This book is copyright protected. This book is only for personal use. You cannot amend,
distribute, sell, use, quote or paraphrase any part, of the content within this book,
without the consent of the author or publisher.

Disclaimer Notice:

Please note the information contained within this document is for educational and
entertainment purposes only. By reading this document, the reader agrees that under
no circumstances is the author responsible for any losses, direct or indirect, which
are incurred as a result of the use of the information contained within this document,
including, but not limited to, − errors, omissions, or inaccuracies.

A CIP catalog record for this book is available from the Library of Congress

ISBN: 978-1-961196-00-1 (Print) ISBN: 978-1-961196-01-8 (E-Book) ISBN:
978-1-961196-02-5 (Hardcover)

Contents

Introduction

Introduction

To all you bluffers and those who have been taken by the Bluff! It's time to say "Bye-Bye" and create a new way of thinking. In this book, you'll learn the art of observation, the power of body language, and how to present yourself confidently... but it doesn't stop there. We'll also dive into the psychology of persuasion and negotiation, teaching you the skills of getting what you want and sealing the deal like a boss! No more "fake it 'til you make it." If you're tired of dealing with a phony, it's time to get the real start on reading people like a pro.

However, let's not forget about the fine art of closing. We'll complete your journey by having you bring all your newfound skills together to take your game to the next level. It's time to stop the Bluff and start winning people over with ease.

I promise to keep you engaged without complicated theories. I will keep it relatable with a touch of witty humor to spark your mind for the possibilities of a new YOU! So, if you're ready to become a master of reading people, then let's get started. Say goodbye to the bluffer of the past and say hello to a whole new level of confidence and success!

1

Chapter 1: The Art of Observation

Look, let's get one thing straight. People are hard to read. They're like these complicated little puzzles we're constantly trying to figure out. And let's be honest, most of the time, we're clueless. But what if I told you there's a way to decode all those hidden messages people send you? A way to understand their feelings or thoughts without them even saying a word? It's called the art of observation, my friend. And let me tell you that it's a foundational skill that can help you win people over, land that dream job, or even ace that first date.

There is a lot of information I will be delivering to you, but don't worry; I've got you covered. I will re-reference some of this information in the later chapters. So, buckle up and get ready to learn the secrets of the subtle art of reading people's body language.

What Do I Mean by the Term "Observation"?

Observation is like a superpower. It's the ability to pick up on subtle cues and signals that most people miss. And when it comes to reading body language, observation is your best friend. When you learn to read body language like a pro, you can tell when someone is nervous, confident, lying, or even attracted to you. It's like having a secret window into their mind.

Now, I know what you're thinking. "But hey, I'm not a mind-reader! How can I know what someone thinks just by looking at their body?" Well, my friend, that's where I come in. The brightest minds in business all use these techniques. I have personally learned from the best, from CEOs to investment bankers, top salesmen, and politicians. I'm here to share my vast knowledge with you. In this chapter, I will teach you the art of observation and help you become an expert reader of nonverbal cues. We'll cover everything from body language basics to subtle signals that can give away a person's true thoughts and feelings.

But before we dive in, I want to clarify this: this isn't some magic trick or mind-reading voodoo. Reading body language is a skill; like any skill, it takes practice. But with the proper techniques and patience, you can read people like a book. So, get ready to say "bye-bye" to bluffers and hello to the truth because we're about to dive into the art of observation.

The Importance of Paying Attention

Look around you. There's a whole world full of people, each with unique personalities, experiences, and stories to tell. But how much attention do you pay to them? How much do you know about the people you interact with every day?

Most of us don't pay much attention to the people around us. We're too busy thinking about ourselves, our problems, and our goals. But paying attention is essential if you want to be successful in life, your relationships, and your career. In all seriousness, paying attention to others is crucial for success in all aspects of life.

Why should you pay attention? Well, for starters, it helps you understand people better. You can pick up on subtle cues and body language that can reveal much about what someone is thinking or feeling, even if they're not saying it outright. Paying attention also helps you build stronger relationships. When you take the time to listen to someone, to understand their perspective and their needs, you can build trust and rapport with them. This can be incredibly valuable in both personal and professional contexts.

But most importantly, paying attention can help you avoid misunderstandings and conflicts. When you can pick up on the nuances of someone's communication, you can avoid misinterpreting their words or actions. This can prevent a lot of unnecessary drama and stress in your life.

Of course, paying attention is easier said than done. We live in a world of distractions, from social media notifications to the constant buzz of our phones. It can be hard to focus on the present moment and tune in to what someone is saying or doing. But the good news is paying attention is a skill that can be developed. With practice, you can train yourself to be more observant and attentive and pick up on the small details that can make a big difference in your relationships and life.

One way to improve your observational skills is to practice mindfulness. Mindfulness involves focusing on the present moment without judgment or distraction. Through regular mindfulness, you can train your brain to be more attentive and focused. Another way to improve your observational skills is to practice active listening. Active listening involves hearing what someone is saying and paying attention to their body language, tone of voice, and other nonverbal cues. By practicing active listening, you can better understand what someone is trying to communicate and respond more effectively.

But perhaps the most important thing you can do to improve your observational skills is to be curious. Curiosity is the fuel that drives observation. When genuinely interested in other people and their experiences, you naturally pay more attention to them. So, cultivate your curiosity, and you'll find that paying attention becomes much easier.

Ultimately, observation is about much more than just reading body language. It's about learning to be present at the moment, to connect with the people around you, and to understand their needs and perspectives. It's about building stronger relationships, avoiding conflicts, and achieving tremendous success in all areas of your life. But don't expect to become a pro overnight. Improving your observational skills is a process that takes time and effort. It requires a willingness to be open and curious and a commitment to practice regularly.

You may also encounter some obstacles along the way. For example, you may find that certain people are more challenging to read than others or that you struggle to stay focused in certain situations. Don't be discouraged by these challenges. Instead, use them as opportunities to learn and grow. Another essential thing to remember is that observation is not a one-way street. Just as you are observing others, they are also observing you. So, be mindful of your body language, tone of voice, and other nonverbal cues. Make sure that your behavior is communicating what you want it to.

Let's say you're at a party, and you've been observing someone for a while, trying to figure out if they're into you or not. You're so focused on observing them that you forget about your body language. So, while trying to look calm and confident, you possibly accidentally spill your drink all over yourself, making you look like a clumsy fool. Then, to make matters worse, you might trip over your own feet while trying to clean up the mess and fall flat on your face.

Meanwhile, the person you were observing was also observing you, and they couldn't help but laugh at your ridiculous antics. You now realize that you've completely blown your chances with them, and maybe you slink away in embarrassment. The lesson here? Always be mindful of your behavior and body language, even when focused on doing the observing, because you could end up looking like the fool yourself!

The art of observation is a valuable skill that can significantly impact your relationships, career, and overall success in life. By paying attention to the people around you, you can better understand their needs, perspectives, and emotions and respond more effectively. So, start cultivating your curiosity, practice mindfulness and active listening, and be present in the moment.

With time and effort, you can become a master observer and achieve tremendous success and fulfillment in all areas of your life. But what happens when the people around you are not saying what they really mean? What if their words are not matching their actions? That's where the skill of decoding nonverbal communication comes into play.

Observing Nonverbal Communication

Nonverbal communication is an art that is mastered with practice, observation, and intuition. It is the process of sending and receiving messages without using words. It includes everything from facial expressions and body movements to the tone of voice and even silence. Research shows that up to 93% of communication is nonverbal! Observing and interpreting nonverbal cues allows you to uncover hidden truths about people and situations.

However, nonverbal communication is not always straightforward. The same gesture or expression can mean different things depending on the context and cultural background. It's essential to be mindful of these differences and consider them when reading nonverbal cues.

Another challenge of nonverbal communication is that people can be skilled at masking their emotions. Have you ever tried to play poker with a mime artist? It's impossible to tell whether they have a good hand because their poker face is always on point! You can't rely on their nonverbal cues because they're so good at masking their emotions. Similarly, some people are good at putting on a poker face and hiding their true feelings, even when their nonverbal cues may suggest otherwise. The only way to beat them is to look for inconsistencies between verbal and nonverbal communication, but good luck getting them to talk!

Furthermore, we should focus on clusters of nonverbal cues instead of one gesture or expression. A single gesture or expression can be misleading, but combining them can provide a more accurate picture of a person's state of mind. For instance, if someone is smiling, but their arms are crossed, and their body is turned away, this could indicate that they are not genuinely happy.

Touch is a powerful form of nonverbal communication. A pat on the back can convey congratulations or support, while a hug can express affection or comfort. However, it's important to remember that touch can be invasive or threatening, so always respect someone's boundaries. Now, let's imagine someone is trying to congratulate their boss by patting them on the back but accidentally striking them so that the boss falls onto their desk! While the intention was to convey congratulations, the force of the touch ended up being invasive and even potentially threatening to the boss. This highlights the importance of being aware of personal boundaries and adjusting the level of touch accordingly.

In addition, nonverbal communication can be influenced by our own biases and preconceptions. We may unconsciously interpret nonverbal cues based on our assumptions and beliefs rather than on the actual meaning behind them. Imagine you're at an event, and you see someone standing in the corner, arms crossed, and with a severe expression. You might assume they're angry or upset, but they're just trying to hold in a fart! When interpreting nonverbal cues, remember that sometimes people's body language might have nothing to do with their emotions or intentions. It's essential to be aware of these biases and approach nonverbal communication with an open mind.

Becoming a pro at reading body language requires practice and honing your observation skills. You can start by observing people in different settings. Identify people's other facial expressions and gestures and what they may mean. Another helpful technique is to ask open-ended questions to encourage people to share more about themselves. This can allow you to observe their nonverbal cues and gain insight into their thoughts and feelings.

Nonverbal communication is not a substitute for verbal communication. Verbal communication provides essential context and clarification to help us better understand a person's non-verbal cues. Therefore, it's necessary to pay attention to both verbal and nonverbal cues and to seek clarification when needed. However, what occurs when there is a mismatch between words and actions? When does a person claim to be joyful but display an unfavorable facial expression or nonverbal cues? Knowing the art of body language is, therefore, essential.

2

Chapter 2: The Art of Body Language

How to Present Yourself with Confidence

L et's face it; we've all been in situations where we feel nervous and anxious about how we're coming across to others. Whether it's a job interview or a first date, our body language can speak volumes about our confidence and presence. If you're tired of feeling like a deer in the headlights during high-pressure situations, it's time to brush up on your body language game. Let's face it, whether trying to make a killer first impression or seal the deal with a potential client, how you present yourself is crucial.

In this chapter, we will discuss the different types of body language, from the subtle cues to the more obvious ones, and I'll help you understand how others can interpret them. You'll learn to control your body language so it works for you, not against you.

But that's not all. You will also learn how to read people like an open book. You will master the subtle nuances of body language.

You'll understand how to use your wardrobe to your advantage, and we'll provide you with some great tips for dressing to impress. In a nutshell, you will be able to present yourself with the kind of confidence that will make people flock to you like moths to a flame.

Understanding the Different Types of Body Language

Reading body language is a complex art, and if you want to master it, you need to understand its different types. Our bodies can communicate a wealth of information, sometimes without realizing it. Some examples of body language are facial emotions, gestures, eye contact, and others. But deciphering these cues can be a challenge. So, let's dive into body language and uncover the secrets.

Facial Expressions

Let's start with the basics. The first type of body language you must know about is Facial Expressions. Our faces are incredibly expressive; even the slightest twitch or shift can convey various emotions. For example, a raised eyebrow can signal surprise or disbelief, while a furrowed brow can indicate anger or frustration. Our faces can express multiple feelings, from joy to sadness, anger to surprise, and everything in between. A simple smile or frown can convey much about a person's thoughts and feelings. For instance, if someone is smiling genuinely, their eyes will also light up, and the muscles around their mouth will create a natural curve.

On the other hand, if someone is forcing a smile, their eyes may appear dull, and the muscles around their mouth may not be symmetrical. This could indicate that the person is not genuinely happy and their smile is just a façade. Understanding these subtle cues can help us decipher a person's emotions and intentions. The way someone looks at you (or doesn't look at you) can tell you a lot about how they're feeling.

Body Movements

Everything we do with our bodies, from motions to stances to how we stroll and pose, is considered a bodily action. Gestures can be both conscious and unconscious, revealing a person's state of mind. For instance, someone who feels confident may stand up straight with their shoulders back and chest out. Conversely, if someone feels anxious or uncomfortable, they may cross their arms, which can signify defensiveness or protectiveness.

From pointing and nodding to waving and shrugging, gestures can add emphasis and meaning to our words. Breathing patterns can also reveal a lot about someone's emotional state. Shallow, rapid breathing can indicate anxiety or stress, while slow, deep breathing can signal relaxation and calmness.

Posture is a critical component of body movement. How someone sits or stands can reveal much about their mood or attitude. For example, slouching can signal laziness or disinterest, while standing up straight can convey confidence and professionalism. Additionally, how people use their hands and arms can reveal a lot about their thoughts and feelings. If someone is excited, they may wave their arms around, while if someone is nervous, they may fidget or play with their hands. Understanding these gestures can help us better understand people's emotions and motives.

Vocal Cues

Another type of body language is **vocal cues**. This includes everything from tone of voice and volume to pacing and inflection. For example, speaking in a monotone voice can indicate boredom or disinterest, while a lively and enthusiastic tone can signal engagement and excitement.

Let's say you're chatting with someone about your favorite topic - ice cream (because who doesn't love ice cream?). If they're responding in a monotone voice, with little inflection or enthusiasm, it's safe to say they're not as excited as you are about the topic. However, if their voice rises in pitch and volume, their pace quickens, and they start sharing their favorite flavors, you've struck a chord. They're interested in the conversation and likely to become a good friend (unless they love vanilla, you might have to reconsider).

Please pay attention to their vocal cues the next time you're conversing with someone. Is their tone flat or lively? Are they speaking softly or loudly? These little indicators can make a big difference in interpreting the conversation. So, tune in, listen up, and read between the lines. You might learn a thing or two about what people are saying and even uncover a mutual love for mint chocolate chips.

Proximity

Proximity is also a type of body language. The distance between two people can reveal their relationship or level of comfort with each other. For example, standing too close to someone can be invasive or threatening, while standing too far away can signal disinterest or discomfort.

Suppose you and a stranger are conversing at a party. If they're standing so close that you can smell their breath, it's safe to say they're invading your personal space. Unless, of course, you're into that sort of thing. On the other hand, if they're standing so far away that you have to shout to be heard, it's safe to say they're not very interested in what you have to say, let alone getting to know you better.

If you're trying to get to know someone, you must find the right balance between standing too close and too far away. It's like a Goldilocks situation, and you need to find the distance that's "just right." So, pay attention to the space between you and others next time you're out and about. Finding the right proximity can make all the difference in the world and help you understand the body language of people around you and the unspoken message they are trying to convey.

Other Factors to Consider About Body Language

Individual differences, such as personality traits or past experiences, can influence body language. For example, someone naturally introverted may exhibit different body language than someone more outgoing or extroverted.

It's important to remember that body language is not an exact science. While some specific patterns and cues can help interpret nonverbal communication, there is no one-size-fits-all approach.

Cultural norms and expectations can also influence body language. For example, in some cultures, avoiding eye contact is seen as a sign of respect, while in others, it can be interpreted as a lack of honesty or interest. Similarly, certain gestures or postures may be seen as offensive or inappropriate in certain cultures, so it's essential to be aware of these differences when interpreting body language. Artifacts, such as clothing or accessories, can also convey information about a person's identity or personality. For example, someone wearing a suit might be perceived as professional or powerful, while someone wearing a band t-shirt might be seen as more casual or laid-back.

One exciting aspect of body language is the concept of leakage. This refers to when someone's body language contradicts their words or intended message, often revealing their true thoughts or feelings. For example, someone might say they're okay while clenching their jaw or avoiding eye contact, indicating they're upset or angry.

Another important aspect of body language is **context**. The meaning of a particular gesture or expression can vary depending on the situation or environment. For example, a smile might indicate happiness in one context but could be a sign of nervousness or discomfort in another.

Lastly, it's important to note that body language can be intentional and unintentional. Some people may use body language as a deliberate means of communication. While others may not be aware of the messages they send through their nonverbal cues.

The Power of Body Language: Communicating Confidence and Presence

You may have heard the saying, "Actions speak louder than words." When it comes to body language, this couldn't be truer. The way you hold yourself, the way you move, and the expressions on your face can all communicate confidence, presence, and authority. Here are some tips to help you harness body language's power and confidently present yourself.

Stand Up Straight

This might seem obvious, but how many people slouch or hunch over when standing or sitting is incredible. Standing up straight makes you look taller and more confident and can also help you breathe easier and feel more energized.

Picture this: you're at a party, feeling like a boss in your new outfit but slouched over like you're carrying the world's weight on your shoulders. Your friend approaches you and says, "Why the long face?" And you're like, "What are you talking about? I'm fine." But your body language is screaming, "I hate this party, and I want to go home." And then you wonder why no one wants to talk to you.

But if you stand up straight like you got a stick up your butt (just kidding, don't do that), suddenly you look more approachable, confident, and attractive. Plus, you can breathe easier.

The next time you feel down in the dumps or need a quick confidence boost, stand up straight and show the world who's boss. And if anyone asks why you're standing so tall, tell them I sent you.

Make Eye Contact

Eye contact is a powerful way to connect with others and communicate confidence. When you're speaking with someone, please make an effort to look them in the eye. This shows you're engaged and interested in what they say.

When talking to someone, you must look them in the eye. I'm talking full-on, laser beam eye contact. Why? Because it shows that you're not afraid. It shows that you're confident, engaged, and interested in what they're saying. It shows you're not some pushover but a force to be reckoned with.

Now, I know what you're thinking. "But what if I'm shy? What if I'm awkward? What if I have a lazy eye?" First of all, stop making excuses. Second of all, let me tell you a little story.

There was once a man named Frank. Frank had a lazy eye. And not just any lazy eye, but a lazy eye that would wander off and do its own thing without warning. It was like having a disobedient child attached to your face. But Frank didn't let that stop him. He knew that eye contact was necessary, so he devised a solution. He started wearing an eye patch. That's right, an eye patch. And not just any eye patch, but a badass pirate eye patch.

And you know what happened? People started looking at him differently. They didn't see a guy with a lazy eye. They saw a guy with a pirate eye patch. And let me tell you, pirates are badass. They don't take crap from anybody. So, the next time you feel insecure about your eye contact, remember Frank and his pirate eye patch. And if all else fails, pretend you're a pirate. Argh, matey!

Smile (but not too much)

A genuine smile can go a long way to making others feel at ease and building rapport. However, be careful not to overdo it. Imagine this: you approach someone and attempt to make a good impression. So, you put on your best smile, saying, "I'm happy to meet you," but it looks insincere. That's not the kind of impression you want to make, right?

So, what do you do? First, relax. Smile like you mean it. Don't be the fake person selling used cars that actually knows nothing about cars. You're bound to be caught with your lying face.

Second, know your limits. In front of the client, if you have no reason to be smiling, then don't! You might look like a plastic doll or a character from a horror film. Instead, focus on your strengths; maybe you can tell a good joke. Maybe you have a deep interest in Science or have a great sense of humor. Use that to your advantage. But please...avoid religion and politics!

But as a secret tip, smiling can create power within when you're alone preparing for a client meeting. Researchers have discovered that the simple act of smiling, even forced laughter, can bring feelings of happiness and reduce stress. There are claims that the mere act of smiling can increase levels of dopamine and serotonin, our body's feel-good hormones.

When you smile, your brain releases tiny molecules called neuropeptides to help fight off stress. The more you smile, the more effective you are at breaking the brain's possibility of thinking negatively. You may end up rewiring your brain to make positive patterns occur more often than negative ones.

Smiling triggers positive emotions, including optimism and confidence. And optimistic, confident salespeople win more and achieve bigger sales. So look in the mirror and give yourself a big Cheshire cat smile to start your day right!

Use Open Body Language

Open body language, such as uncrossed legs and arms, can communicate that you're approachable and receptive. On the other hand, closed body language, such as crossed arms or legs, can make you appear defensive or unapproachable.

So, picture this: you're at a party and see someone you'd like to talk to. You walk over to them, and what do you see? They cross their arms and legs. Oh boy, here we go. They're sending you a clear message: "Back off; I'm not interested in talking to you." And you know what? Unfortunately, you'll probably never know if you could have changed their mind. It's a terrible feeling being shut down before you even have a chance to try.

Now, let's flip the script. You're at that same party and see someone you'd like to talk to. You walk over to them and notice their arms and legs are uncrossed; they're smiling and making eye contact. Aren't they saying, "Hey there, I'm friendly and approachable? Come on over, and let's have a chat." And you know what? You're probably going to take them up on that offer. Who doesn't like a warm welcome?

Body language can make all the difference when communicating confidence and presence. If you want to be approachable, open yourself up. Literally. Keep your arms and legs uncrossed, and you'll send a message saying, "I'm open to conversation." If you want to come across as defensive or unapproachable, cross those arms and legs. But don't say I didn't warn you when you're left standing there all by yourself.

So, folks, pay attention to your body language next time you're out. And if you're feeling particularly naughty, mess with people a little bit. Cross your arms and legs, and watch as they shy away from you like you're a porcupine. Then, uncross them and watch as they flock to you like you're the life of the party. It's like magic, folks—body language magic.

Use Hand Gestures (but not too much)

Hand gestures can be a great way to emphasize your points and communicate enthusiasm. Hand gestures can add emphasis to moments and make them more memorable. But you've got to be careful not to go overboard.

I mean, picture this: You're trying to make a serious point about the state of the economy, and suddenly, you're doing jazz hands like a Broadway performer. Your audience will be more focused on your weird hand movements than on what you're saying. Make no mistake; hand gestures are used by the world's most potent and influential people. They will usually choose one or two specific gestures and use them accordingly. From the Queens wave to Bill Clinton's thumb pointing, these gestures are used to emphasize a point.

So, the lesson here is to use hand gestures sparingly and make them count. Don't be afraid to use them, but keep it simple and accurate, and for the love of God, no jazz hands.

Avoid fidgeting

Fidgeting, tapping your foot, or playing with your hair can make you appear nervous or unconfident. Look, we've all been there before. You're in a high-pressure situation, like a job interview or a first date, and suddenly, your leg starts bouncing up and down like a hyperactive kangaroo on crack. Or you could begin twirling your hair around your finger like a lovesick teenager from a cheesy rom-com. Whatever your fidget of choice may be, it's not doing you any favors in the confidence department.

Let's face it: fidgeting makes you look like your body is scream-ing, "I'm nervous, and I don't know what to do with my hands!" And let's be honest: Nobody wants to hire or date someone who always looks nervous.

So, what's the solution? Please take a deep breath and focus on staying still, my friend. I know, easier said than done. But trust me, it's worth it. Think of yourself as a majestic oak tree, firmly rooted in the ground and unshakable in the face of any storm.

And if all else fails, bust out some wild dance moves. Who knows, your potential employer or date will be so impressed by your sick dance skills that they'll forget about your nervous fidgeting. Or they'll think you're a weirdo. Either way, it's worth a shot, right?

Use Power Poses

Power poses, standing with your arms raised in a "V" shape or standing with your hands on your hips, can help boost your confidence and make you feel more powerful. Before your big meeting, you can prepare with this skill privately, maybe in the office bathroom or in front of your bedroom mirror, to gain power. And no, it's not by drinking Red Bull or doing a hundred push-ups before your big meeting. Stand like Superman or Wonder Woman and instantly feel like a badass.

I'm not kidding; it's Science. Standing with your arms raised in a "V" shape or standing with your hands on your hips sends signals to your brain that you're in charge. So, next time you feel nervous or unsure of yourself, pose like you're about to save the world from an alien invasion. Your coworkers will say, "Whoa, that person means business."

Or imagine you're at a job interview and feeling a bit intimidated by your potential boss. Suddenly, you bust out the power pose, and they say, "Wow, this person is a confident badass; we need them on our team!"

Just be careful not to overdo it. You don't want to come off as too aggressive. Keep it cool, keep it casual, and keep it powerful. So, there you have it, folks—the power pose: the ultimate weapon in your quest for confidence and dominance. Now go forth and conquer! And don't forget to strike a pose before you do.

Pay Attention to Your Tone of Voice

Your tone of voice can also communicate confidence and presence. Speak clearly and avoid speaking too quickly or too quietly. A strong, confident voice can help you command attention and make a lasting impression. Your tone of voice is like a superhero's outfit; it can either make you look badass or like a clown. So, speak clearly and avoid talking like you've got a mouthful of marbles. You don't want people asking you to repeat yourself all the time or, worse, ignore you altogether.

A strong, confident voice can do wonders. It can make you sound like a leader, boss, king, or queen. Don't get too carried away; there's a thin line between sounding confident and like a douchebag. So, use your powers wisely, my friends.

Imagine you're at a party, seeing a hot babe or a handsome dude wanting to strike up a conversation. You go over there and start talking like you're trying to break a world record for the fastest-talking human being. They will think you're either on drugs or just plain nuts.

On the other hand, if you talk so slowly, they will get bored and move on to the next person.

So, what's the solution, you ask? Well, it's simple. Speak at an average pace. You don't need to rush or drag out your words like you're in a damn Shakespeare play. Just talk like you would to your friend or your grandma. Trust me, it works.

The Power of Dressing for Success: Using Clothing to Communicate Confidence

How we dress can significantly impact our body language and, in turn, our overall confidence and communication with others.

Dressing for success can not only make us feel more confident, but it can also change the way others perceive us. When we dress professionally and put together, we send a message that we take ourselves seriously and are ready to take on any challenge.

This increased confidence can translate into stronger body language, such as better posture and bold gestures. By understanding the power of dressing for success and using it to our advantage, we can improve our body language and communicate with greater confidence and authority.

You have heard the saying "Dress for success," but have you ever wondered why it's so important? The truth is the way you dress can have a powerful impact on how you feel and how others perceive you. This section will explore the power of dressing for success and how you can use clothing to communicate confidence.

Dress For the Occasion

The first rule of dressing for success is to dress appropriately for the occasion. Whether it's a job interview or a networking event, ensure your outfit is appropriate for the setting. There's a fine line between dressing for success and looking like an idiot.

I remember having a job interview at a fancy law firm once. I thought, "I got to look sharp for this one." So, I put on my best suit, slicked back my hair, and walked in there like I owned the place. But as soon as I walked in, I realized I had made a grave mistake. Everyone else was wearing jeans and T-shirts! I felt like a total fool in my over-the-top suit. It was like showing up to a pool party in a three-piece suit. Yeah, you look fancy, but you'll be sweating your ass off while everyone else is having fun.

So, the lesson here is simple: dress appropriately for the occasion. If you're going to a job interview, find out what the company dress code is and follow it. If you're attending a networking event, wear something professional that shows your personality. And if you're not sure what to wear, ask! It's better to ask and be sure than to show up looking like a clown. Trust me; I've been there. And it's not a good look.

Invest In Quality Clothing

Quality clothing not only looks better, but it also lasts longer. Investing in quality pieces that fit well and flatter your body can make a big difference in how you feel and how others perceive you.

Investing in quality clothing is not only a smart financial decision but can also boost your confidence and make you feel like a million bucks. You don't have to break the bank to do it, either. Just look for pieces that fit well and flatter your body. And if you're not sure what to buy, ask for help! Don't be afraid to ask a salesperson for their opinion. They're there to help you, not judge you. And if they do judge you, well, forget them. You're the one with the quality clothes that last longer. So, invest in yourself and your wardrobe. Trust me; it's worth it. And who knows, you'll even get a compliment or two. Try not to let it go to your head, okay?

Choose Colors That Flatter Your Skin Tone

Specific colors can make you look washed out or tired, while others can make you look vibrant and alive. Experiment with different colors to find what works best for you. Let me tell you a little story. Once, I wore a bright yellow shirt to work, thinking I would look like a ray of sunshine. But instead, I looked like a walking highlighter. My coworkers were practically wearing sunglasses to avoid the glare.

On the other hand, I once wore a deep forest green shirt, and suddenly, everyone told me how healthy I looked. I didn't suddenly become a fitness guru overnight, but the color made me look more vibrant and alive. So, experiment with different colors to find what works best for you. Don't be afraid to try something new and bold. You may discover a new power color that makes you feel like a superhero. But remember, there's a fine line between bold and obnoxious. You don't want to be that person who looks like a walking rainbow. Unless that's your thing, then, by all means, rock it.

Embrace Your Style

Dressing for success doesn't mean you have to sacrifice your style. Embracing your style can help you feel more confident and comfortable in your clothing. Just because you're dressing for success doesn't mean you must give up your style. It would help if you embraced it like a long-lost lover.

I remember having a job interview once, thinking, "I got to look professional." So, I wore this stuffy suit and collared shirt that made me feel like a snake was strangling me. I walked into that interview looking like a robot, and guess what? I didn't get the job. But then, I had another interview and said, "Screw it, I'm going to wear something that makes me feel like a badass." I put on my favorite leather jacket, jeans, and boots. And you know what? I got the job!

So, embrace your style. It can make you feel more confident and comfortable in your clothing. Just make sure it's appropriate for the occasion. You don't want to be that person who shows up to a wedding wearing a t-shirt and shorts (unless it's a beach wedding, then go for it). And remember, fashion is all about expressing yourself. So, if you want to wear a neon green tutu to work, then go ahead and rock it. Just make sure you're ready for the compliments (and the stares).

Don't Forget About Grooming

Grooming is just as important as the clothing you wear. Ensure your hair is styled, your nails are trimmed and clean, and your shoes are polished. Now, I know some of you think, "I don't need to groom; I'm a natural beauty." But let me tell you something, even the most beautiful flower needs a little pruning to look its best.

So, make sure your hair is clean and styled. Don't walk into that job interview looking like you just rolled out of bed (even if you did). And don't forget about your nails. You don't want to be shaking hands with someone and have them notice your dirty talons.

Finally, let's talk about shoes. Listen, people are going to judge you based on your shoes. It's just a fact of life. So, make sure they're clean, polished, and looking sharp. Don't be someone who walks into a room, and everyone thinks, "Man, those shoes look rough."

Remember, grooming is just as important as the clothing you wear. So, make sure you're looking your best. And who knows, you'll even get a compliment or two (or someone will mistake you for a movie star).

The Art of Mirroring: How to Build Rapport with People

First things first, what is mirroring? Mirroring is imitating the body language, tone, and speech patterns of the person you're talking to. It might sound weird, but it's a natural way to build a connection with someone. When you mirror someone, you create a sense of familiarity, making the other person feel comfortable and at ease.

Now, let's talk about how to mirror someone effectively. The key is to be subtle. You don't want to come across as a creepy copycat. Start by matching the person's body language. If they're leaning forward, you lean forward, too. If they're crossing their legs, you do the same. If they're nodding their head, you nod too.

Next, match their tone of voice. If they're speaking softly, lower your voice, too. If they're sputtering, speed up your speech. If they're using hand gestures, use them too. The goal is to create a sense of synchronicity with the person you're talking to.

It's important to note that mirroring is not about mimicking someone. It's about building rapport and creating a connection. You don't want to be a carbon copy of the person you're talking to. Instead, focus on subtle mirroring that shows you're paying attention to them and are on the same wavelength.

One thing to keep in mind is that mirroring is not a one-size-fits-all technique. You have to adapt to the person you're talking to. If someone is reserved, you don't want to come on too strong with your mirroring. If someone is animated, you want to match their energy.

Another critical aspect of mirroring is being aware of your body language. You don't want to mirror someone's negative body language. For example, if someone is crossing their arms, it might be a sign that they're closed off or defensive. You don't want to mirror that body language, which could create a hostile atmosphere. Instead, combat their crossed arms by maybe leaving your arms open and slightly leaning towards them with a smile. This will keep the focus on mirroring positive body language.

Mirroring is also an excellent tool for building trust. When you mirror someone, you create a sense of empathy and understanding. It shows that you're paying attention to and caring about what they say. This can be especially helpful in professional settings, where building trust is crucial for success.

It's important to note that mirroring is not a magic bullet. It's just one tool in your arsenal for building connections with people. You still have to be genuine and authentic in your interactions. It will come across as disingenuous if you're mirroring someone without genuinely listening to them or being interested in what they have to say.

Let's talk about some situations where mirroring might not be appropriate. For example, you don't want to mirror that negative energy if someone is angry or upset. Instead, you want to try to diffuse the situation with positive body language and a calm tone of voice. Additionally, if someone has a speech impediment or a physical disability, mirroring might not be appropriate.

Body language is a powerful tool that can help you communicate confidence, presence, and authority. You can project confidence and make a lasting impression by dressing outrightly, standing up straight, making eye contact, using open body language, and practicing power poses. So, the next time you're in a high-pressure situation, take a deep breath, stand up straight, and let your body language talk.

You may think that body language is all you need to project confidence and authority, but let me tell you, my friend, it's only half the battle. Because while your body is busy communicating, your words are doing the heavy lifting. Words can inspire, per-suade, and captivate. Words can make people fall in love or start a war. Words can change your life. That's why, in the next chapter, we will explore the power of words and how you can use them to win people over. But be warned, this is not your average language lesson. We will dig deep into the dirty secrets of persuasion, the tricks of the trade, and the art of manipulation. So, buckle up, my friend, because things are about to get interesting.

3

Chapter 3: The Power of Words

How to Be A Great Communicator

D o you know that one person who always seems to have the perfect comeback or argument? They could sell a ketchup popsicle to a woman in white gloves. What's their secret? It's simple: the power of words. In this chapter, we'll explore the art of verbal communication, the importance of active listening, and how to understand and respond to subtext.

Choosing the right words and tone can make all the difference in how your message is received. Words are like weapons - choose them wisely, and you can conquer the world. But choose them poorly, and you might as well be shooting blanks.

So, if you want to become a master of words, keep reading. You will be equipped with the tools you need to win people over with your words, charm, and wit. Just remember, with great power comes great responsibility. Please don't abuse your newfound abilities; you may lose people instead of winning them over.

Active Listening: The Key to Effective Communication

So, you want to be a good communicator. Do you want to impress people with your words and convince them to do things your way? Well, guess what? It's not about what you say but how you listen. That's right, folks. The key to effective communication is active listening. And no, I don't mean just nodding your head and pretending to care while you secretly think about what you will eat for lunch.

Active listening means fully engaging with the person you're talking to. It means paying attention to their words, tone, and body language. It means putting aside your thoughts and opinions and trying to understand their origin.

Now, I know what you're thinking. "But hey, I'm already a great listener. I hear people all the time!" I hate to break it to you, but hearing is just the act of perceiving sound. Listening is the act of actively trying to understand and interpret that sound. And trust me, many people out there are great at hearing but terrible at listening.

How Do You Become an Active Listener?

Well, for starters, you need to focus. When you're having a conversation, don't let your mind wander. Don't start thinking about what you will say next or how you will respond. Just be present in the moment and give the person your full attention.

Let me give you an example. So, the other day, I was talking to my friend, and he was telling me about his new job. I was nodding along, pretending to listen, but I was already planning my response in my head. I would tell him about this cool thing I did at work last week.

Anyway, he must've noticed that I wasn't listening because he suddenly stopped talking and said, "You're not even listening to me, are you?" And I was like, "No, I am! You were talking about your job, right?" And he was like, "No, dumbass. I was talking about my new dog."

So, the story's moral is don't be like me. Please focus on the person before you and listen to what they're saying. Otherwise, you might talk about your friend's new job when he's telling you about his new furry friend.

Another essential aspect of active listening is asking questions. Don't just assume that you understand what the person is saying. If you're not sure, ask for clarification. And don't be afraid to dig deeper. Ask open-ended questions, encouraging the person to elaborate and share more of their thoughts and feelings.

Of course, asking questions is only half the battle. It would help if you also listened to the answers. Too often, people ask questions and immediately start thinking about their response before the other person has even finished speaking. Don't be that person. Listen to the entire answer before formulating your response.

Let's say you're talking to your friend about their new job. They tell you about their boss and how he's always making weird noises during meetings. Instead of pretending to be interested, ask them, "What kind of noises are we talking about here? Is he like a walrus or a seal or something?" And when they answer, try not to laugh too hard; otherwise, they might think you're making fun of them. Remember, asking questions shows that you care and want to understand the other person. Keep it accurate, my friends.

And speaking of responses, let's talk about validation. When someone shares their thoughts or feelings with you, acknowledging them is essential. You don't have to agree with everything they're saying. Still, you should validate their perspective and show that you understand where they're coming from. Validation can be as simple as saying, "I can see how you would feel that way," or "That's a valid point." It's small but can make a huge difference in how the other person perceives you and the conversation.

Overcoming Obstacles and Finding Success in Active Listening

Now, let's get real for a minute. Active listening isn't always easy. In fact, sometimes, it can be downright difficult. You may not agree with the person's words, or you're not interested in the topic. Whatever the case, pushing through those barriers and staying engaged is essential.

One trick that can help is to practice empathy. Try to put yourself in the other person's shoes and understand why they feel like they do. Even if you disagree, you can still empathize with their perspective and show them you care about their feelings.

And let's not forget about nonverbal communication. When listening to someone, your body language can speak just as loudly as your words. Make eye contact, nod your head, and use other nonverbal cues to show your engagement and interest in the conversation.

But wait, there's more! Active listening isn't just about being present in the moment. It's also about being mindful of your own biases and assumptions. We all have our own experiences and beliefs that can color how we interpret and respond to what others are saying. It's essential to be aware of these biases and try to set them aside when actively listening.

For example, let's say you're conversing with someone with a different political view than you. You might be tempted to shut down or dismiss their perspective immediately. But if you want to be an effective communicator, you need to be able to listen to and understand all viewpoints, even if you disagree with them. So, take a deep breath, set aside your biases, and approach the conversation with an open mind. You might be surprised at what you learn.

Here's a pro tip: if you're struggling to stay engaged in a conversation, try repeating what the other person says. This not only shows that you're actively listening, but it also helps to reinforce the information in your mind. For example, if someone tells you, "I'm frustrated with my job right now," you could respond with something like, "It sounds like work has been challenging for you lately." This not only shows that you're actively listening, but it also helps the other person feel heard and validated.

But let's not forget about the power of silence. Sometimes, the best thing you can do as an active listener is to be quiet and let the other person talk. Don't feel like you have to fill every moment with words or responses. Sometimes, just listening can be the most powerful thing you can do.

And finally, don't forget to follow up. After a conversation, take a few moments to reflect on what was said and what you learned. There may have been areas where you could improve your listening skills or things you could have done differently to make the other person feel more heard.

Following up also shows you care about the conversation and the other person's perspective. It can solidify the connection and lead to more productive and meaningful conversations in the future.

So, there you have it, folks. Active listening is the key to effective communication. It's not about what you say but how you listen. By focusing on the other person, asking questions, practicing empathy, and setting aside your biases, you can become a more effective communicator and build stronger, more meaningful relationships with those around you.

But what happens when the person you're trying to communicate with isn't saying what they mean? What if their words are just a cover for deeper emotions and thoughts? This is where the importance of understanding and responding to subtext comes into play. Sometimes, the true meaning behind a person's words can be buried beneath layers of hidden meaning, and it takes a skilled communicator to uncover them.

Misunderstanding and miscommunications can occur without recognizing subtext, leading to missed opportunities. So, the question remains: Do you have what it takes to understand and respond to subtext?

Understanding and Responding to Subtext

We've all had those moments when talking to someone, and we can't quite pinpoint why their words seem off. It could be a feeling in our gut, a shift in our tone, or a phrase that seems out of place. Whatever it is, there's likely something more going on beneath the surface. That something is subtext.

Subtext is the underlying message or meaning behind someone's words. It's the unspoken thoughts and emotions conveyed through tone, body language, and the choice of words. It's what makes conversations complex and nuanced and separates a great communicator from a mediocre one.

So why is subtext important? If you want to truly understand and connect with others, you need to be able to read between the lines. You need to be able to pick up on the subtle cues and signals that reveal what someone is thinking or feeling. And once you understand the subtext, you can respond in a way that shows empathy, builds trust, and strengthens your relationships.

But How Do You Become a Subtext Detective?

It starts with paying attention. You must be fully present, listening carefully to what someone is saying and how they're saying it. You need to observe their body language, facial expressions, and tone of voice. And it would help if you were willing to ask questions and clarify what they mean.

Of course, picking up on subtext isn't always easy. People are complex creatures, and their subtext can be just as difficult. It might take some practice, but you can become a pro at reading between the lines with time and patience.

One way to start honing your subtext skills is to pay attention to a person's words. Often, the words someone chooses can reveal much about their thoughts and emotions. For example, if someone says, "I'm fine," but their tone is flat and their body language is closed off, they might not be okay. They might be upset, angry, or frustrated. You can better understand what they're feeling by paying attention to their words, tone, and body language.

Another example could be when you ask someone if they want to hang out, and they say they're busy. Instead of taking their words at face value, look at their tone and body language to determine if they're not interested. If that's the case, you could respond by saying, "No problem, maybe we can plan something for another time," instead of pushing the issue.

Sometimes, subtext can be positive. For instance, if your partner says, "I love you," with a big smile and a warm hug, the subtext is clear - they love you. Responding to this subtext might involve reciprocating the sentiment or expressing gratitude for their affection.

On the other hand, if your partner says, "I love you," with a monotone voice and an unenthusiastic hug, the subtext might indicate that they don't mean it. Responding to this subtext might involve asking your partner how they're feeling and trying to understand why they're not expressing their love more genuinely.

Subtext can also be present in written communication, such as emails or texts. For example, if someone responds to your message with a short, curt answer. The subtext might indicate that they're annoyed or upset with you. In this case, responding to the subtext might involve asking if everything is okay and offering to discuss any issues.

Important Aspect of Responding to Subtext

It's important to note that subtext can be tricky - sometimes, it's unclear what someone is trying to communicate. In these cases, asking for clarification or expressing that you're unsure what they mean is okay. It's better to have an open and honest conversation than to make assumptions based on unclear subtexts.

A critical aspect of responding to subtext is to avoid getting defensive. If someone's subtext indicates that they're upset with you, it's natural to feel defensive or attacked. However, staying calm and listening to what they're trying to communicate is essential. Responding to the subtext defensively or aggressively will only escalate the situation and make it harder to resolve.

Another critical factor in understanding and responding to subtext is awareness of your subtext. What are you trying to communicate when you say something? Are you using subtext to avoid expressing your feelings or manipulating someone into doing what you want? Awareness of your subtext can help you communicate more authentically and avoid misunderstandings.

Verbal Communication: Choosing the Right Words and Tone

Words have immense power. They can inspire, motivate, and persuade people. They can also hurt, offend, and damage relationships. In verbal communication, the right words and tone can make all the difference in how our message is received. The words we choose can convey different meanings, and using them appropriately is essential. Choosing the right words requires careful consideration of the message's context, audience, and purpose.

How To Choose the Right Words

Understanding your audience is essential when selecting the right words. Who are you communicating with? What is their background, age, and level of education? Knowing this information will help you tailor your language to be more relatable and understandable to your audience or the individual. Using too complex words for your audience can make your message unclear. On the other hand, using words that are too simple can make you come across as condescending.

So, let's say you're talking to your grandma. She's old and wise, but she didn't go to college. You don't want to throw around words like "juxtaposition" or "antithesis" 'because she may not know what you're talking about. Instead, use words like "compare" and "opposite." That way, she'll be able to follow what you're saying without potentially feeling dumb.

Now, let's say you're talking to your little cousin. He's in elementary school and still learning his ABCs. You don't want to talk down to him either 'because that will make you look like a jerk. But you also don't want to use words he's never heard of. Instead of saying, "I'm going to the grocery store to procure some sustenance," say, "I'm going to the store to get some food." See how easy that was?

Secondly, consider the context in which you'll be communicating. Are you trying to convey a serious message or lighten the mood with some humor? Are you speaking to someone or a group professionally or with a friend? Your word choice should reflect the tone of the situation. Using slang and informal language might be appropriate when chatting with friends. But it might be unprofessional in a business setting.

Now imagine this - you're in a job interview, trying to impress the interviewer with your fancy vocabulary. You start talking about how you're a "garrulous communicator with exceptional loquacity," and the interviewer's face turns from interested to confused. You might think you sound smart, but you're confusing the hell out of the person in front of you.

On the other hand, if you're hanging out with your friends, you can't go around sounding like a Shakespearean actor. You must keep it accurate and relatable and use words your friends understand. Imagine saying, "My dear companions, would you fancy partaking in a soirée at my humble abode?" to your buddies and watching them look at you like you spoke a different language.

The bottom line is knowing your audience and choosing your words accordingly. Unless you're purposely trying to make people laugh, save the slang and informal language for your buddies. In a professional setting, keep it classy and avoid sounding like a teenager texting their crush.

Thirdly, avoid filler words and phrases. Words like "um," "like," and "you know" can make you sound uncertain or unprepared. Take a moment to collect your thoughts before speaking, and choose your words intentionally. This will help you express more confidence and credibility. Nobody likes a bumbling, uncertain speaker. You know, the kind that fills every other word with "um" or "like" or "you know." It's like, do they even know what they're talking about? Do they have a point, or are they just wasting everyone's time?

Think about what you want to say, and then say it with intention. Choose your words like you choose your clothes: carefully and with purpose. Because here's the thing: when you speak confidently and clearly, people are likelier to listen to you. They'll respect you. They'll think, "Wow, this person knows their stuff." And who doesn't want that?

So, take a beat the next time you're about to launch into verbal diarrhea of filler words. Pause for a second. And then, when you're ready, unleash the power of your words with all the force of a thousand suns. Or, you know, try not to sound like a total dweeb. Either way works.

How To Choose the Right Tone

The purpose of your message determines the tone you choose to use. For instance, if your goal is to persuade, you will use a different tone than if your goal is to inform. The right tone can make your message more convincing. The tone of your message is just as important as the words you choose. The tone sets the emotional context for your message and can affect how your audience receives it.

It's essential to consider how your audience will respond to different tones and choose the one that best matches your message's purpose. The same message delivered to different audiences may require different tones. It's essential to consider how your audience will likely respond to different tones. For instance, a calm, reassuring tone can help soften the blow if you deliver bad news.

The tone of your message should match its purpose. An enthusiastic and upbeat tone can be effective if your goal is to inspire or motivate. On the other hand, if your goal is to convey empathy, a calm and understanding tone may be more appropriate.

Now, let's get real here. Imagine convincing your boss to let you take a week off to go to Disneyland. While using a firm tone, you can't just say, "Hey, boss, I want to go to Disneyland. Can I have a week off?" No, no, no. You've got to use your words wisely and your tone even wiser. Calmly and meekly, try something like, "Hey boss, I know I've been busting my butt lately, and I was wondering if there's any way I could take a week off to recharge my batteries. And hey, if you're feeling adventurous, you could come too, and we could ride some rollercoasters together!"

See the difference? The right tone can make your message go from meh to yeah, baby! So, don't go all chipper like a cartoon character if you want to be taken seriously. And if you want to be relatable, don't go all formal like you're writing a research paper.

Imagine a scenario where you're in a high-stakes conversation, trying to convey your message to someone critical to your success. You've listened actively, understood the subtext, chosen the right tone, carefully selected your words, and crafted a clear message. But as you speak, you notice that the other person seems distracted, their eyes wandering around the room.

How can you ensure that your message gets across effectively? How can you persuade someone without coming across as manipulative or deceitful? The answer lies in understanding the psychology of persuasion. By tapping into people's emotions, needs, and desires, you can subtly influence their behavior and make them more receptive to your message. But be warned, the power of persuasion can be both a blessing and a curse, and if used recklessly, it can have disastrous consequences. So, if you want to master the art of persuasion and win people over. It's time to delve into the secrets of "The Psychology of Persuasion."

4

Chapter 4: The Psychology of Persuasion

How to Win People Over

Welcome to the world of persuasion, my dear friend. Whether you realize it or not, you're constantly being persuaded. From the ads you see on TV to the conversations you have with your friends, persuasion is all around us. And let's face it; some people are better at it than others.

But here's the good news: persuasion is a skill that can be learned. And in this chapter, we're going to show you how. We'll explore the psychology behind persuasion, from the science of influence to the power of social proof. We'll also dive into the art of framing and the principle of reciprocity, two techniques that can help you build trust and credibility with anyone.

So why bother learning how to persuade others? Well, for starters, it can make your life much easier. Whether you're trying to sell a product, get a promotion at work, or convince your spouse to go on vacation, knowing how to win people over can help you achieve your goals.

But here's the thing: persuasion isn't about being manipulative or deceitful. It's about understanding what motivates people and using that knowledge to build connections and foster relationships. It's about being honest, authentic, and empathetic. And that's what you'll see in this chapter.

So, get ready to take your persuasion skills to the next level. Whether you're a seasoned salesperson or a complete novice, we've got something for everyone. And you might even learn something about yourself. So, buckle up, and let's get started on this journey together.

The Science of Influence: Understanding the Psychology Behind Persuasion

Persuasion is the art of convincing others to see things your way, and it's a skill that can be developed and honed. Understanding the psychology behind persuasion can help you more effectively influence others, whether in personal or professional settings. The factors influencing persuasion are crucial in determining how successful we are in convincing others. These factors include the audience's beliefs, values, emotions, and cognitive biases. By understanding these factors, we can tailor our approach and message to effectively appeal to our audience, increasing the likelihood of success. Let's look at some of these factors below;

Scarcity

When resources are restricted, people prefer to place a higher value on what remains. This is why phrases like "limited time offer" or "while supplies last" can be so effective in marketing. By creating a sense of urgency, you can persuade people to act quickly before missing out on something.

Have you ever noticed how you're more inclined to buy something when it's labeled as a "limited time offer" or "while supplies last"? Who wouldn't want to get their hands on something before it's too late?

Well, my friends, let me tell you something. This is all due to the magic of scarcity. It's a basic human instinct to value things more when they're scarce or in limited supply. It's like that last slice of pizza at a party - everyone wants it because they know it won't be around for long.

Now, imagine this scenario. You walk into a store and see a sign that reads, "Only 10 left in stock!" Suddenly, you feel a sense of urgency creeping up on you. You start to panic, thinking about all the people who might snatch up the remaining items before you can get to them. It's like a battle royale for that last item on the shelf.

But let's take it up a notch. Imagine if that same store also had a sign that said, "Only 10 left in stock - and they're magical!" Now, my friends, we're talking about a new level of scarcity. Who wouldn't want to get their hands on a magical item before they all go? You could be the envy of all your friends - or the subject of their ridicule.

Scarcity is a powerful tool when it comes to persuasion. Whether it's a limited-time offer or a magical item, the fear of missing out can drive people to act quickly. So next time you see a sign that says "while supplies last," remember that you're not just buying a product - you're buying into the psychology of persuasion. And if that product happens to be magical, well, that's just a bonus.

Authority

It is easier to gain people's confidence and cooperation if you present yourself as an authoritative figure or subject matter specialist. For example, if you're trying to convince someone to trust you on a medical matter, it helps if you're a doctor. If you're trying to convince someone to listen to your legal advice, it helps if you're a lawyer. You get the point.

If you want to persuade someone to do something, you better have some authority under your belt. And no, I don't mean just being bossy pants or a know-it-all. I'm talking about being an actual expert in the field.

But here's the thing, sometimes, people use their authority to persuade you to do ridiculous things. Like, have you ever been to a chiropractor? They'll crack your back like a glow stick and tell you it's good for you. And you know what? People believe it. Why? Because they're an authority figure in the world of spinal cracking.

Or how about those beauty influencers on social media? They tell you that putting snail slime on your face will make you look ten years younger. And you know what? People buy it. Why? Because they're an authority figure in the world of slathering goo on your face.

Likability

People are more likely to comply with requests from people they like and trust. Building rapport, being friendly, and finding common ground can all help to increase likability and make persuasion more effective.

Let's say you want your friend to lend you their car for the weekend. You can't just stroll up to them and say, "Hey, give me your car. I want to take it for a spin." No, no, no. That's not how it works. It would help if you buttered them up a bit. Find out what they like and what makes them tick. Maybe they're into yoga, hiking, or eating pizza. Whatever it is, find something in common and bond over it.

Once you've established a connection, it's time to turn on the charm. Be funny, be witty, and be yourself (unless you're a total jerk, in which case, try being someone else). Make them laugh, smile, and feel good about themselves. Compliment them on their hair, outfit, or music choice. And for Goodness sake, don't be a suck-up. Nobody likes a brown-noser.

Now, here's the tricky part. You need to make your request without sounding like a needy little leech. You can't say, "Hey, can I borrow your car for the weekend because I don't have one, and I want to impress this girl I met on Tinder." That's a recipe for disaster. Instead, try something like, "Hey, I was wondering if you'd be cool with letting me borrow your car for the weekend. I promise to take good care of it, fill the tank, and return it in one piece. What do you say?"

See, that's not so hard. Being likable increases your chances of getting what you want. And if all else fails, offer to buy them a pizza. Works every time.

Consistency

Despite changing their minds, people are notorious for continuing to act based on their prior beliefs. This is why getting someone to make a small commitment, such as signing up for a newsletter, can increase the likelihood that they will later comply with a more significant request.

Let's say you want your friend to join your knitting club. You can't just go up to them and say, "Hey, join my knitting club; it's going to be awesome!" They'll probably say, "Uh, no thanks, I'm good."

But if you start small and ask them to sign up for your knitting newsletter, they might be more likely to say yes. Then, when they start getting those sweet knitting tips and tricks in their inbox, they'll feel like they're already part of the knitting community. And before you know it, they'll show up to your knitting club meetings with bells on.

The funny thing is that once someone commits to something, they're likelier to stick with it. It's like they don't want to let themselves down or something. So, use that to your advantage, my friends. But remember, don't use this power for evil. Only use it for good, like getting your friends to join your knitting club or something.

Emotions

If you want to be the ultimate influencer, you got to know how to play with people's emotions like a damn fiddle. Emotional appeals and logical arguments often persuade people. I'm talking about tapping into their deepest desires for love, acceptance, and happiness. Think about it, when was the last time you bought something just because it looked cool? Or because you thought it would make you look cool? Advertisers know this all too well, so they use emotional appeals to sell their products.

Take perfume commercials, for example. They don't just show you a bottle of fancy-schmancy fragrance and tell you it smells nice. Nah, they offer you a couple in love, running through a field of flowers, laughing and hugging each other. And then they hit you with that tagline, "Because love is in the air." Boom. Sold.

Or what about those fast-food commercials that show you juicy burgers and crispy fries? They don't just tell you it tastes good; they show you a group of friends having the time of their lives, bonding over burgers and fries. And then they hit you with that tagline, "Come hungry, leave happy." Cha-ching.

So, if you want to be a master influencer, you got to tap into people's emotions. Make them feel something. And if you can make them laugh, even better. Just don't make them cry unless you're selling tissues.

Incentives

Offering a reward or incentive for complying with a request can increase the likelihood of someone doing so. However, ensuring the incentive is relevant and desirable to the person you are trying to persuade is essential. What do they value? What do they find desirable? What makes them tick? Once you have a handle on that, you can craft the perfect incentive to seal the deal.

Imagine trying to convince your friend to go on a diet with you. You could try the guilt-tripping approach, but we all know how that ends. So, instead, you offer your friend a reward for every pound they lose. You take them to their favorite movie every time they lose a pound. That's right, folks. For every pound they lose, you can sit through your least favorite movie.

And just like that, you've convinced your friend to go on a diet with you. It's a win-win situation. They get to indulge in their favorite movie and lose weight simultaneously. And you get to have a diet buddy. It's the power of incentives, my friends. So, remember the power of incentives next time you're trying to convince someone to do something. Make it relevant and make it desirable.

Repetition

Repeating a message or argument can reinforce it and make it more memorable. However, it's important not to overdo it, as too much repetition can lead to annoyance and resistance.

Think about it. Have you ever had that one friend who constantly repeats the same story every time you hang out? You know, the one about how they almost became a professional cheese sculptor but ended up selling insurance instead? Yeah, that guy. Don't be that guy.

But, on the other hand, a little repetition can go a long way. It can reinforce your message and make it stick in people's minds. For example, let's say you want to convince your friend to see that new superhero movie with you. You could say, "Hey, you should see this movie with me. It's got explosions, car chases, and superpowers. It's going to be epic." And then, a few days later, you could say something like, "Remember that movie I told you about? We should see it. I heard it's breaking box office records." See what I did there? I repeated my message, but I didn't overdo it.

So, my friends, remember this: repetition can be a powerful tool in persuasion. But use it wisely. Don't be that annoying guy who won't shut up, and don't be that forgetful guy who can't remember what he said five minutes ago. Be the cool guy who uses repetition to get what he wants without driving people crazy.

You know that feeling when you're trying to convince someone of something, but they don't seem to be getting it? It's like banging your head against a brick wall. You try every factor in the book, but nothing works. Well, my friend, I hate to break it to you, but it's not always about the argument. That's right; sometimes, it's all about the framing. What's that, you ask? It's how you present your idea - the context, background, and setting.

And let me tell you, it can make all the difference. If you want to be persuasive, you need to know how to frame your argument in a way that speaks to your audience. And believe me, it's not as easy as it sounds. So, buckle up, my friend, because we're about to dive deep into the world of framing - and things are about to get real.

The Power of Suggestion: Planting Seeds of Agreement

The power of suggestion is a force to be reckoned with. It's like planting a seed of agreement in someone's mind and watching it grow into a full-fledged idea. It's a technique that can influence people without them even realizing it. And when it comes to closing a deal, it can be the difference between success and failure.

How To Use the Power of Suggestion

So, what is the power of suggestion? It's the art of subtly introducing an idea or thought into someone's mind without them feeling like they're being manipulated. It's about planting a seed of agreement and letting it grow independently. And it's a technique that can be used in various situations, from sales to negotiations.

It's important to remember that the power of suggestion is not about tricking people or being dishonest. It's about using language and communication persuasively and effectively. It's about finding common ground with the other person and using that to build a connection and make them feel comfortable.

Be Subtle

You don't want to come across as pushy or manipulative. Instead, you want to be gentle and persuasive. You want to make the other person feel like the idea is their own, not something you're trying to force upon them.

For instance, you've been trying to sell your car to your buddy. You've utilized the negotiation skills you learned and even offered a few discounts as a sign of compromise. But your friend is still hesitant. Well, it's time to get subtle. Being pushy or manipulative is a surefire way to ruin a friendship and lose a potential buyer.

Instead, you want to be gentle and persuasive. You want to make your friend feel like buying your car is their idea. And how do you do that? By dropping subtle hints here and there. Start by mentioning how great your car has been for you and how it has never let you down. Then, casually mention how you're considering getting a new car soon but are not in a hurry to sell.

Next, mention how you saw a similar car for sale online and were considering checking it out. Your friend will naturally want to know more about this other car, and that's when you drop the bomb: "Well, I'm not sure if I'm ready to let go of my car just yet. But if you're interested, maybe we could work something out?"

Boom. Your friend will always think it was their idea to buy your car. And you'll walk away feeling like a subtle persuasion. Ensure you don't accidentally drop a "buy my car, damn it" in the middle of the conversation. Subtlety is key, my friend.

Use Questions

By asking the right questions, you can plant ideas in someone's mind without them realizing it. For example, if you're trying to sell a car, you could ask, "Don't you think this car would look great in your driveway?" This simple question plants the idea that the car would look good in their driveway without directly asking them to buy it.

Don't be too obvious about it, okay? You don't want to come off as a used car salesman or something. Keep it subtle, like a ninja planting an idea in someone's mind. So go ahead, kiddos, and try it out. Who knows? You may be the next big salesperson, making deals left and right with your sneaky little questions.

Storytelling

By telling a story that supports your idea or product, you can plant the seed of agreement in someone's mind. For example, if you're trying to sell a product that saves time, you could tell a story about how someone else who used the product saved them time and allowed them to get more done in their day. This story plants the idea that the product is useful and valuable without directly saying it.

So, you want to tell a story to convince someone to buy your product? Well, let me tell you a story about my friend... Dan was always running late. He'd be late for meetings, late for dinner, late for his funeral if he could be. But one day, Dan stumbled upon an innovative product that changed his life. It was a time-saving gadget that allowed him to get things done quickly.

After using this product for a short period of time, he was always on time, always organized, and always in control. His friends were amazed, and even his arch-nemesis Bob, who was never late for anything, was impressed. So, if you want to be like Dan and impress your friends and even your arch-nemesis, you should buy this product. It's called a watch! It's not magical, but it sure feels like it.

Be Confident

If you're unsure of yourself or your product, it will show in your language and body language. But if you're confident and believe in what you're saying, that confidence will come across and make the other person more likely to agree with you.

Let's say you're trying to sell your friend the idea of getting a pet llama. You've done your research, know all the benefits of owning a llama, and feel pretty confident. But as soon as you start talking to your friend, your confidence disappears faster than a llama on roller skates. You start stuttering, can't remember any of the benefits, and accidentally call the llama a "dolphin" thrice in a row. Your friend looks at you like you've lost your mind. "What are you talking about? Llamas aren't even aquatic animals!" Then he turns and walks away, shaking his head.

Now, let's rewind and try that again. This time, you walk up to your friend, shoulders back, head held high. "This may sound crazy, but you should get a pet llama. They're low-maintenance, they're great with kids, and they'll even protect your house from burglars. Plus, have you seen those adorable little ears? I mean, come on."

Your friend looks at you skeptically, but you're not fazed. You know you're right and are not afraid to show it. "Trust me on this. You won't regret it." Your friend still isn't convinced, but they can't deny you're one confident llama-lover. They agree to think about it, and you walk away feeling like you could sell a llama to a dolphin.

Be Patient

The power of suggestion takes time to work. You can't expect someone to agree with you immediately. But if you plant the seed of agreement and give it time to grow, you'll be more likely to see results.

Have you ever tried convincing a friend to watch a movie you thought was amazing, but they wouldn't budge? Yeah, it's frustrating. But the key to persuasion is patience. You can't force your friend to watch the movie; that'll make them more resistant. Instead, you must plant the seed of agreement and let it grow.

So, how do you do that? Well, start by mentioning the movie in passing. Talk about how much you enjoyed it or how it's been getting great reviews. Then, drop it for a bit. Let your friend think about it on their own. If they don't bring it up again, don't worry. Just keep mentioning it every once in a while. Eventually, they'll start to think it was their idea to watch the movie, not yours.

But remember, be patient. This process takes time. You can only expect your friend to agree with you after some time. But if you keep planting the seed of agreement, eventually, it'll sprout, and they'll be begging you to watch the movie with them. So, don't be pushy the next time you're trying to convince someone of something. Plant the seed and let it grow. With patience, you'll be able to persuade anyone of anything (well, almost anything).

Be Aware of Your Audience

Different people respond to different types of language and communication. Some people respond better to facts and figures, while others respond better to emotion and storytelling. By understanding your audience, you can tailor your approach and use the power of suggestion more effectively.

For example, let's say you're trying to convince your friend Bob to come to a party with you. If Bob is the type of guy who loves facts and figures, you might tell him about all the statistics that show how going to parties can improve your social life and reduce stress levels. But if Bob is more of an emotional guy, you might tell him about how you went to a party and had the time of your life and how it changed your perspective on social events.

Knowing your audience is critical. If you're trying to persuade a group of scientists to fund your new research project, you'll want to come equipped with all the data and research to back up your claims. But if you're trying to persuade a group of teenagers to try a new product. You'll want to focus on the emotional benefits and how it will make them feel. For example, if you're trying to convince them to buy a new energy drink, you might emphasize how it will give them the energy they need to stay up all night gaming with their friends.

Ultimately, it all comes down to understanding your audience and catering your message to their preferences. It's not about manipulating or tricking people but rather about finding the right way to communicate your message in a way that resonates with them. So, next time you're trying to win someone over, consider what kind of message will work best for them. And if all else fails, bring out the funny cat videos – everyone loves those.

The Art of Framing: How to Shape Perceptions

The art of framing is a technique that can help you shape perceptions and win people over. With the right framing, you can make even the most negative situations seem cheerful, and the most complex ideas seem simple. Are you ready to learn how to wield this powerful tool? Let's dive in!

First things first, what is framing? Framing is selecting and emphasizing certain aspects of an idea, situation, or message to influence how it is perceived. It's like putting a frame around a picture – the frame shapes how we see the image, just like framing how we see an idea or situation.

Framing is all about perspective. When you frame something, you choose the perspective you want others to see. This is why framing is such a powerful tool – it allows you to control how people perceive things. And let's be honest; controlling how people perceive things is the key to winning them over.

Let me ask you this: have you ever taken a selfie? Of course you have! Don't even lie to me. When you took that selfie, did you hold the camera up high to make yourself look thinner, or did you hold it down low to make yourself look taller? Yeah, you get where I'm going with this.

Framing is the same thing. It's like taking a selfie of an idea or situation. You choose the angle that makes it look the best. And let's face it, who doesn't want to look their best? I know I do.

So, if you're trying to convince someone of something, you want to make sure you're framing it in a way that makes you look good. It's like putting on your best outfit before a first date. You want to show your best side.

But here's the thing, if you're trying to convince someone to do something that's not in their best interest, you should rethink your framing strategy. For example, let's say you want your friend to eat a bug. Yeah, I know, gross, but go with me here. You could frame it as a dare, like "I bet you can't eat this bug!" or you could frame it as a health food, like "This bug is packed with protein and essential nutrients!" See what I did there? So, the key to successful framing is to choose the proper perspective. And, of course, to not be a jerk and try to convince people to eat bugs. That's just gross.

How Can You Use Framing To Your Advantage?

Let's start with the basics. The first step is to identify what you want to frame. Is it an idea, a situation, or a message? Once you've identified what you want to frame, the next step is to figure out how you want to frame it.

You can use a few different types of frames, depending on what you're trying to achieve. For example, you can use a gain frame, which emphasizes the benefits of a particular idea or situation. Or you can use a loss frame, emphasizing the negative consequences of not taking a specific action.

Another type of frame is the temporal frame, which emphasizes how an idea or situation will play out over time. For example, you might use a long-term temporal frame to highlight the long-term benefits of a particular action or a short-term temporal frame to emphasize the immediate benefits.

Of course, it's not just about choosing the right type of frame – it's also about the language you use to frame things. The words you choose can significantly impact how people perceive things. For example, if you want to emphasize the benefits of a particular action. You might use words like "opportunity," "potential," and "advantage." On the other hand, if you want to emphasize the negative consequences of not taking action, you might use words like "risk," "threat," and "consequence."

Things To Consider Before Framing Any Perspective

It's important to remember that framing isn't about lying or deceiving people. It's about presenting information in a way that highlights certain aspects and downplays others. You're not changing the facts but influencing how people perceive them.

One of the most important things to keep in mind when it comes to framing is that different people respond to different frames. What works for one person might not work for another. This is why it's so important to know your audience. What are their values? What motivates them? What do they care about? Once you know these things, you can choose the right frame to win them over.

But it's not just about knowing your audience – it's also about knowing yourself. What are your own biases and assumptions? What frames do you tend to use? Are there any frames that you're particularly good at using? By being aware of your tendencies, you can be more deliberate and strategic in your framing.

Another thing to keep in mind is that framing is not a one-time thing. It's an ongoing process. It would help if you were constantly monitoring how your frames are being received and adjusting them as necessary. This requires being open to feedback and adapting your approach as needed. It's also important to be aware of the frames others use in case someone else is framing the situation to your disadvantage.

Social Proof: The Power of Using the Influence of Others to Your Advantage

Have you ever bought something just because everyone else was buying it? Or have you ever been swayed to try a new restaurant because it had a long line outside? Congratulations, my friend, you've been influenced by social proof. Social proof is the idea that people are more likely to do something if they see others doing it. This is why testimonials, reviews, and social media influencers can effectively persuade people to buy a product or try a service. If other people are doing and enjoying it, it must be worth doing, right?

What Is Social Proof?

Social proof is a powerful psychological phenomenon when people look to others for guidance on behavior. We all want to make the right decisions and look to others for validation. If we see that many people are doing something, we assume it must be the right thing. Social proof can be used in various situations, from marketing and advertising to personal interactions. By understanding the power of social proof, you can use it to your advantage and easily win people over.

It's a fact that we humans are so easily influenced by what others are doing. I mean, think about it. If most people wear a certain clothing style. We automatically assume it must be cool and rush to buy it ourselves. If we hear about a trendy new restaurant, we're all over it like white on rice.

That's just the science of influence at work. We're wired to look to others for guidance on what to do and not do. And it's not just limited to fashion and food, oh no. It extends to everything from the products we buy to the beliefs we hold.

Take, for example, the case of the infamous Tide Pod Challenge. For those of you who don't know, a bunch of teenagers decided it would be a great idea to eat laundry detergent pods because they saw other people doing it on the internet. And before you knew it, the Tide Pod Challenge went viral and became a full-blown phenomenon.

Now, you might be thinking, "Who in their right mind would eat a Tide Pod?" But that's the thing - when you see enough people doing something, no matter how stupid it might seem, it starts to look normal. It starts to look like something you should be doing, too.

One of the most common forms of social proof is testimonials. When we see that other people have had a positive experience with a product or service, we're more likely to try it ourselves. This is why companies often include customer testimonials on their website or advertising. But social proof goes beyond just testimonials. It can also be seen in the way we dress, the music we listen to, and even the books we read. We're all influenced by the behavior of others, whether we realize it or not.

Have you ever driven by that popular nightclub and noticed the long line of beautiful people waiting to get in? Well, could it be that the club owner is purposely letting people in slowly to maintain the long line, or perhaps there are paid actors and models standing in the line? People drive by thinking it's a hot spot filled with all gorgeous people, making them want to be a part of it.

The power of social proof is most evident in group settings. When we're in a group, we're more likely to conform to the group's behavior. This is why people often do things in a group they wouldn't do alone. Social proof isn't just limited to marketing and advertising. It can also be used in personal interactions. If you're trying to persuade someone to do something. You can mention that other people have already done it and had positive results. This will make them more likely to follow suit.

How To Harness the Power of Social Proof in Various Settings

If you want to use social proof to your advantage, you must understand its psychology. People are more likely to be influenced by social proof when they're unsure what to do or don't have enough information to decide.

Create A Sense of Scarcity and Competition

When people see that something is in high demand or that only a limited number of items are available, they're more likely to act quickly. Also, when people see that others compete for something, they're more likely to want to compete. So, companies that use phrases like "limited time offer" or "today only" in their advertising are creating a sense of scarcity competition.

Celebrity Endorsement

When we see a celebrity using a product or service, we're more likely to want to use it ourselves. This is why companies often pay celebrities to endorse their products. But celebrity endorsement can be a double-edged sword. If the celebrity gets into trouble or does something controversial. It can reflect poorly on the product or service they endorse. So, if you use celebrity endorsements, choose your celebrity wisely.

Building a feeling of belonging

When people feel like they're part of a group or a community, they're more likely to be influenced by the behavior of others in that group. This is why companies often create online communities or forums for their customers. When people feel like they're part of something bigger than themselves, they're more likely to be influenced by the behavior of others in that group.

That's why we find companies always try to create communities and forums for their customers. They want you to feel like you are part of a tribe of people who all love their product or service. It's like a secret handshake that only members of the club understand.

So, if you're trying to persuade someone to do something, try to build a feeling of belonging first. Start a club for people who like to eat pizza for breakfast (I'm kidding, don't do that). Or create a Facebook group for people who love your product. Just make sure you're not being too obvious about it. Nobody likes to feel like they're being manipulated.

Build Trust and Credibility

If you want people to trust you and your ideas, you can mention that others have already endorsed them. Also, if people see that others have already had a positive experience with something. They're more likely to trust it themselves. This is why companies often use customer reviews and ratings on their websites.

For example, if you're giving a presentation, you can mention that other experts in your field have also supported your ideas. But be careful not to overuse this social proof technique. If people feel like you're relying too heavily on the opinions of others. They may start to question your expertise and authority.

Highlight The Popularity of Something

If you're trying to convince someone to try a new restaurant, you can mention that it's always busy and people love it. This will make them more likely to want to try it themselves. For example, you could tell your friend, "This place is so popular; they're giving away free bibs to all the droolers waiting in line." Or, "The only downside to this restaurant is that you might have to elbow a few people out of the way to get a table. That's just the price you pay for good food."

Create A Sense of Exclusivity

When people feel like they're part of an exclusive group or have access to something others don't, they're more likely to value it. When we see others doing or loving something, we're more likely to do it or appreciate it, too. But when we feel like we're part of an exclusive group or have access to something others don't, it's like we're part of a secret club. And who doesn't love a secret club?

Let me give you an example. Do you know those fancy, schmancy restaurants with a long waiting list to get in? You know, the kind where you have to dress up like you're going to prom just to eat some overpriced steak? Yeah, those places. They're all about exclusivity. And guess what? It works. People are willing to shell out big bucks to be part of that exclusive club. They feel special, like they're part of something that not everyone can access.

But let's be honest here. It's not like the food is any better than the mom-and-pop shop diner down the street. It might even be worse. But that doesn't matter because people are willing to pay for the experience of feeling special. And that's the key: creating an experience that makes people feel part of something exclusive.

So, if you want to influence people, create that sense of exclusivity. Make people feel part of something special, even if it's not all that special. You may be selling a product or service or trying to get people to come to your party. Whatever it is, make people feel like they're part of an exclusive club. Just don't forget to deliver on your promise, or you might end up with many angry customers.

The Principle of Reciprocity: How to Build Trust and Credibility

In simple terms, reciprocity means that when someone does something nice for us, we feel compelled to return the favor. It's a basic human instinct, and it's one that you can use to your advantage in all kinds of situations.

There is the idea that people feel obliged to repay others when they receive something from them. Think about the last time someone did something nice for you. Maybe they complimented you, helped you with a task, or bought you a gift. How did it make you feel? Chances are, you felt grateful and happy. And if that person were to ask you for a favor in the future, you'd be more than willing to help them out.

That's the power of reciprocity. By doing something kind for someone else, you create a sense of obligation in them. They feel they owe you something in return, even if they don't realize it. And when you need their help or support, they're much more likely to come through for you.

Things to Keep in Mind When Practicing Reciprocity

The principle of reciprocity is about building genuine relationships based on trust and mutual respect. If you only do nice things for people because you want something in return, that will not be sustainable in the long run. People will see right through your ulterior motives, and they'll be less likely to trust you in the future.

But if you approach reciprocity with a genuine desire to help others. You'll find building solid relationships with people much more effortless. When you do something nice for someone else without expecting to get something in return, they'll be more likely to trust you and see you as reliable and trustworthy.

I'm not saying you should buy people new cell phones all willy-nilly. But offering someone something of value, even if it's something small, can make them more likely to do what you want. It's like you're making a down payment on their compliance.

For example, let's say you want your friend to help you move. You could ask them outright, but that might not be enough. Instead, you could bring them a pizza or a six-pack of their favorite beverage. By doing something nice for them, you're activating their reciprocity instinct, and they'll be more likely to say yes to your request.

Critical Aspects of Practicing Reciprocity

But here's where things get interesting. Reciprocity doesn't always have to be equal. Sometimes it's better if it's not. If you do something nice for someone, they might feel like they can never repay you, so they won't even bother trying. But if you do something small for them, they'll feel like they owe you something, and that can be enough to get them to comply with your request.

Another critical aspect of reciprocity is timing. If you want to build trust and credibility with someone, you need to be strategic about when you give and when you receive. If you always take from others without giving anything back, people will resent you and see you as selfish.

But if you're always giving without ever allowing others to reciprocate. You can create an uncomfortable power dynamic for everyone involved. People want to feel like they can contribute to your success and well-being just as you contribute to theirs.

So, the key is to find a balance. Give freely and generously when you can, but also allow others to help you when they can. This creates a sense of mutual dependence and trust for building solid relationships.

One thing to remember when practicing reciprocity is that it doesn't always have to be a grand gesture. Small acts of kindness can be just as effective in building trust and credibility. A sincere compliment, a thoughtful gesture, or a simple "thank you" can go a long way in making someone feel appreciated and valued.

The key is to be consistent in your efforts. Don't just do something nice once and then forget about it. Make a habit of regularly showing gratitude and kindness to the people around you. Over time, these small acts of reciprocity will add up to create a robust foundation of trust and respect.

It's also important to be authentic in your approach to reciprocity. Don't try manipulating people into doing things for you with flattery or insincere compliments. People can sense when you're fake, which will only damage your credibility in the long run.

Instead, be honest and genuine in your interactions with others. If you appreciate something they've done for you, let them know. If you're struggling with something and need their help, be upfront. People will likely trust and respect you when you approach reciprocity with honesty and authenticity.

So, next time you need to persuade someone to do something, remember the power of reciprocity. Offer them something of value, even if it's just a compliment or a funny meme, and watch as they become putty in your hands. Just don't overdo it, or they might start to feel like you're trying too hard. And nobody likes a try-hard.

Congratulations, you are halfway through "Bye-Bye Bluffer." If you've read this far, you are on your way to really hone your skills. The journey to reading people's body language and winning them over can be a long ride. But let me ask you this: what happens when facing a tough negotiation? When the person you're trying to persuade isn't so easily swayed? When you're up against a wall, with nothing but your wit and charm to get you what you want? Trust me, my friend; it won't be a walk in the park. But don't worry, I've got you covered. In the next chapter, we'll dive into the art of negotiation - the skills you need to get what you want, even in the most challenging situations.

5

Chapter 5: The Art of Negotiation

How to Get What You Want

Welcome to the real world, where nothing comes easy. This chapter will explore the ins and outs of getting what you want. This chapter will teach you to set your goals and know your limits before negotiating. How can you expect to get it if you don't see what you want? And if you don't know your limits, you may agree to something you regret later. So, it's essential to take some time to think about what you want and what you're willing to give up.

Once you know what you want, it's time to build rapport with your opponent. Establishing a connection with them will make overcoming objections, finding common ground, and reaching a compromise easier. Remember, you're not trying to win a war here. You're trying to find a win-win solution.

Speaking of compromise, that's the real art of negotiation. It would be best to give a little to get a little. But don't be a pushover, either. Stick to your goals and limits, and be open to creative solutions. Who knows? You might come up with something that's better than what you originally wanted. And finally, when you've found that win-win solution, it's time to close the deal. Getting to yes is the ultimate goal, but don't forget to dot your i's and cross your t's. Make sure everything is spelled out clearly and in writing. You don't want any surprises down the line.

The Importance of Preparation: Setting Goals and Knowing Your Limits

Negotiation can be a daunting task, especially if you're not prepared. Setting goals and knowing your limits is crucial to any negotiation. The importance of preparation cannot be overstated, as it lays the foundation for a successful negotiation. Don't forget that one vital aspect of negotiation is being prepared to walk away if necessary. If the other party isn't willing to meet your goals or respect your limits, sometimes the best option is to cut your losses and move on. Being prepared to walk away can also give you more leverage during negotiations.

Set Clear and Specific Goals

First and foremost, it's essential to set clear and specific goals for the negotiation. What do you want to achieve? What's the best-case scenario, and what's the worst-case scenario? A clear understanding of your own goals will help you focus on what's essential and prevent you from getting sidetracked.

However, it's essential to remember that negotiation is a two-way street. You can only focus on your goals by considering the other party's. Understanding their goals and motivations can help you find common ground and reach a mutually beneficial agreement.

Let's say you're negotiating with your parents for a later curfew. Your best-case scenario is to stay out all night partying with your friends, and your worst-case scenario is to be grounded for life. Staying out all night sounds like a lot of fun, but let's be realistic here. It's not going to happen. You must consider what you want and consider what the other person wants. It's like trying to do the cha-cha by yourself. It just doesn't work.

So, you need to understand what your parents want. Maybe they want you to be safe and responsible. Well, guess what? You want that too! You don't want to end up in the hospital or jail. So, find some common ground and work from there.

Knowing Your Limits

In addition to setting your goals, it's essential to set your limits. What are you willing to compromise on, and what's non-negotiable? A clear understanding of your limits can help you avoid making concessions you'll regret later on.

At the same time, it's essential to be flexible and open-minded during negotiations. Sometimes, what you thought was non-negotiable may not be as crucial as you initially thought. Being willing to consider alternative solutions can help you reach the best outcome.

Let's say you and your lover are negotiating about where to go on vacation. You've set your goal: a relaxing beach getaway. But what about your limits? Are you willing to compromise on the location? Are specific amenities non-negotiable?

Maybe you are dead set on staying at a resort with a swim-up bar, but your partner is convinced that a rustic cabin in the woods is the way to go. It's time to have a serious discussion about your limits. But here's the thing: sometimes, our limits aren't as clear-cut as we think. You may be willing to give up the swim-up bar for a private hot tub. Your partner may be willing to compromise on the cabin if there is hiking nearby.

Being open-minded and flexible during negotiations can lead to unexpected and hilarious outcomes. You may end up in a treehouse on a beach somewhere. The point is to be willing to consider alternative solutions, even if they seem a little crazy at first. Just remember: set your goals, know your limits, and keep an open mind. And if all else fails, flip a coin. Hey, it works for me.

Do Your Research

Another crucial aspect of preparation is doing your research. You need to know as much as possible about the other party, their interests, and their negotiating style. This information can help you anticipate their moves and develop a more likely-to-succeed strategy.

Let me tell you a story to illustrate this point. Once upon a time, there was a guy named Joe. Joe had a job interview with a fancy-pants company. Joe thought he was the bee's knees and didn't need to do any research beforehand. Like a James Bond character, he showed up in his bow tie and tuxedo, thinking that would impress them. Spoiler alert: it didn't.

Joe sat down with the hiring manager, who was a total hard-ass. She asked him tough questions, and Joe had no idea how to answer. He didn't even know exactly what the company did! He just mumbled some nonsense and hoped for the best.

Long story short, Joe didn't get the job. He went home, cried into his vodka martini (shaken, not stirred), and realized that he had messed up big time.

The moral of the story? Do your research. Don't be like Joe. Find out everything you can about the person or company you're dealing with. What are their interests? What are their weaknesses? All of this information can help you devise a plan of attack. So, to succeed in life, start preparing like your future depends on it because it does.

Building Rapport: Establish a Connection with Your Opponent

Is negotiation all about getting what you want? No, it isn't! To succeed in negotiation, you need to start by building rapport with your opponent. Rapport is all about establishing a connection with the other person. It's about finding common ground and building trust. When you have rapport, your opponent is more likely to be open to your ideas and suggestions. This section will explore some of the best ways to build rapport with your opponent.

Be Authentic

The first step in building rapport is to be authentic. People can tell when you're not genuine, which is a huge turnoff. Don't try to be someone you're not. Instead, be yourself. Let your personality shine through. When you're authentic, people will feel more comfortable around you.

Let me give you an example. I once knew a guy who was trying to impress a girl he had a crush on. He decided to take her on a fancy date to a restaurant he couldn't afford. He ordered a meal he had no idea how to pronounce and spilled it all over his shirt. Smooth move, buddy.

I'm not saying you can't take risks when building rapport, but trying to be someone you're not is a recipe for disaster. Instead, be yourself. Let your personality shine through. If you're a jokester, crack a few jokes. If you're a gardener, talk about your favorite flowers.

When you're authentic, people will feel more comfortable around you. They'll see that you're not trying to pull a fast one on them, which can go a long way in building a connection.

So, the next time you're trying to build rapport with someone, remember to keep it accurate. And if all else fails, tell them a funny story about the time you spilled food all over yourself on a first date. It's a great icebreaker.

Show Respect

Showing respect is another important aspect of building rapport. Treat your opponent with respect, even if you disagree with them. Be courteous. You're more likely to receive respect in return when you show respect.

Imagine you're in a heated debate with someone in a crowded room. You're both so passionate about your beliefs that you feel like you're about to explode. Suddenly, the person stops mid-sentence and says, "Excuse me, do you mind if I take a quick bathroom break?" You reply with a nod, still fuming inside. When they return, you notice a piece of toilet paper stuck to the bottom of their shoe. Now, what do you do? Do you point it out in front of the crowd and embarrass them, or pull them aside and privately tell them?

Here's the thing: If you choose to embarrass them, you may lose their respect. On the other hand, if you decide to be considerate, you are still a respected voice in the discussion at hand. Showing respect is like investing in a long-term friendship. It may not give you immediate returns but will pay off in the long run. And who doesn't want a long-lasting relationship? Remember, you may lose a battle, but winning the war is better.

So, remember to be respectful the next time you find yourself in a debate. And who knows, maybe you'll make a new friend by saving them from walking around with toilet paper on their shoes.

Use Humor

Humor is a great way to break the ice and build rapport. It shows that you're not taking yourself too seriously and can help put your opponent at ease. Just be careful not to overdo it. You don't want to come across as unprofessional. Plus, not everyone has the same sense of humor. What you find funny might not be funny to someone else. So, use humor wisely. And if you're unsure if something is funny, run it by a friend or colleague first. And if all else fails, remember this: a smile goes a long way.

Use Active Listening

Active listening is a powerful tool for building rapport. It means paying attention to what your opponent is saying and asking questions. When you show that you're genuinely interested in what they have to say, it helps create a connection.

Let me tell you about my friend Dave. Dave is a terrible listener. The guy couldn't listen if his life depended on it. Whenever I try to converse with him, he constantly interrupts, talks, or ignores me. It's like trying to have a conversation with a brick wall.

Now, I don't want to be too hard on Dave. He's a good guy but doesn't know how to listen. And that's a shame because listening is a powerful tool in building rapport. When you show that you're genuinely interested in what someone has to say, it helps create a connection.

Take my friend, Tim, for example. Tim is a great listener. Whenever we have a conversation, he's always asking questions, showing interest, and engaging with what I'm saying. And you know what? We have a real connection because of that. I feel like he cares about me and what I have to say.

So, if you want to build rapport with someone, you've got to learn how to listen. And I don't mean just sitting there nodding your head and pretending to listen. I mean listening and paying attention to what the other person is saying, asking questions, and showing true interest.

Use Their Name

Using someone's name is a great way to build rapport. It shows that you're paying attention and value them as individuals. Just be careful not to overdo it. You don't want to sound like a used car salesperson.

You know the type - the ones who say your name so often you feel like you're in a horror movie. "Hey there, Bob. How's it going, Bob? You're looking good today, Bob." Ugh, it's enough to make you want to run screaming into the night.

So, when you're trying to build rapport, use their name sparingly. Think of it like seasoning—a little sprinkle here and there is all you need. And don't forget to mix it up. Using their name in every other sentence is not only annoying but also creepy.

If you want to connect, try using something other than their name. You notice they're wearing a cool watch or funky shoes. Comment on that. "Hey, those are some sweet kicks you've got there." It shows you're paying attention and that you're interested in them as a person.

Find Their Motivation

Understanding your opponent's motivation is critical to building rapport. What do they want out of the negotiation? What are their goals? When you know their motivation, you can tailor your approach to better suit their needs.

Imagine you're negotiating with a toddler who wants a piece of candy. You could say, "No, you can't have any candy." And what's the toddler's response? A tantrum. But what if you understood their motivation? What if you knew that the toddler just wanted a taste of something sweet? You could say, "Okay, you can have a piece of candy after you eat your broccoli." And just like that, you've avoided a meltdown.

Of course, negotiations aren't always as simple as dealing with a toddler. But the principle remains the same. You need to understand your opponent's motivation. What do they want? What are their goals? And when you know their motivation, you can tailor your approach to suit their needs.

So, if you're negotiating with your boss for a raise, don't just barge in and demand more money. Understand their motivation. They may be concerned about the company's budget, or they may want to see more effort from you. When you know what they're looking for, you can make a compelling case for why you deserve a raise.

In short, building rapport is all about understanding your opponent. It's about putting yourself in their shoes and seeing the situation from their perspective. When you do that, you'll be able to connect with them and negotiate more effectively. And who knows? You can avoid a tantrum or two along the way.

Be Respectful, and Don't Be Too Aggressive

Treat your opponent with respect and show that you value their opinion. This can go a long way in building a connection and establishing trust. Being too aggressive or confrontational can put your opponent on the defensive and make it difficult to establish a connection. Be assertive, but also be respectful and open to their perspective.

Picture this: you're in a heated argument with your arch-nemesis; let's call him Joe. Joe is a smug know-it-all who thinks he's always right. Now, the last thing you want to do is be too aggressive and start a war. Instead, take a deep breath and channel your inner Buddha.

Show Joe some love, man. Tell him you appreciate his point of view. Let him know that you value his opinion (even though it's as valuable as a screen door on a submarine.)

Being assertive is essential, but being respectful is even more critical. Don't be a jerk, even if Joe deserves it. Don't be confrontational, even if he's a pain in the ass. Keep your cool and stay focused on the task at hand.

If you can do that, my friend, you'll be well on your way to building a connection with your opponent. And who knows, maybe you'll make a new friend.

Show Gratitude and Be Patient

Show gratitude if your opponent does something you appreciate, such as compromising on a point. This can help build goodwill and strengthen the connection between you. Building rapport takes time, so don't rush the process. Be patient and take the time to establish a genuine connection with your opponent.

So, how do you show your gratitude? You could start by giving them a sincere thank-you, maybe even a handshake or a pat on the back. You could offer them a drink after the debate. (Just ensure you don't get so drunk that you start agreeing with them on everything. That defeats the whole purpose.)

Overcoming Objections: How to Address Concerns and Win People Over

Negotiating can be challenging. It can feel like you're constantly battling against the other person, trying to prove your point and get what you want. But it doesn't have to be that way. Negotiating can be an art, a dance between two parties that ends in a win-win situation.

One of the keys to successful negotiation is learning how to overcome objections. Objections are concerns that the other person has about your proposal. They might be worried about the cost, the feasibility, or the potential risks. Whatever the objection, it's your job to address it and win them over. Here are some steps to overcoming objections to win people over.

Understanding The Perspective of The Other

You must put yourself in the other person's shoes and try to see things from their perspective. What do they worry about, and What are their top concerns? What is their desired outcome from this negotiation? So put yourself in their shoes. No, not literally, unless you have the same shoe size as them, in which case, that's just weird.

Anyway, the point is that you need to understand where they're coming from. It's like figuring out why your dog keeps barking at the vacuum cleaner. Maybe he thinks it's a giant monster. Or perhaps he wants to play fetch with it. Who knows? But seriously, folks, if you're going to overcome objections, you need to address their concerns head-on. Don't just dismiss them or try to talk over them.

Listen to what they have to say, and then respond in a way that shows you understand where they're coming from. This involves paying close attention to what the other person is saying, asking clarifying questions, and restating their concerns in your own words to ensure that you understand them correctly.

Prepare For Argument Based on Their Perspective

Alright, we're getting into some severe negotiation territory now. Once you've identified their objections, it's time to prepare for them. To overcome these specific objections, you'll need to have a deep understanding of your proposal and be able to provide evidence to support it. This might involve sharing previous client case studies, statistics, or testimonials. Anticipate what they might say and come up with responses that address their concerns. You want to be ready to counter their objections with compelling arguments that support your proposal.

You must put on your thinking caps and prepare to play defense. It's like a game of verbal dodgeball, except instead of balls, they're throwing objections at you. So, the first step is to anticipate what they might say. Think about it like predicting the weather, except instead of rain or snow, it's objections. Will they say, "It's too expensive"? "We've had a bad experience with similar proposals in the past"? "I don't like your face"? Okay, maybe not that last one, but you get the idea.

This is where you whip out your best arguments and comebacks. You want to be like a verbal ninja, deflecting objections left and right with your compelling arguments and logic.

Stay Calm and Confident

Please don't get defensive or dismissive of their concerns. Instead, acknowledge their objections and show that you understand where they're coming from. This will help to build trust and rapport between you and the other person.

For instance, when someone comes at you with a concern or objection, your instinct might be to get defensive. "What do you mean it won't work? It's foolproof! You're the fool!" But hold up, cowboy. Take a deep breath and put on your best empathetic face.

Use The "Feel-Felt-Found" Method

This involves acknowledging the other person's feelings, sharing how others have felt in the same situation, and then explaining how you or someone else has successfully found a positive outcome to the initial objection.

First, you acknowledge their feelings. Like, "I understand how you feel; I do." Then, you share how others have felt the same way, like, "Others have felt the same concern you have." Finally, you explain how you or someone else has successfully found a positive outcome to the initial objection, like, "But what they found was that after trying it, they loved it!" Boom, objection overruled. Now, if only we could get toddlers to eat their damn vegetables using this method.

Be Flexible

It's also important to be flexible when responding to objections. If the other person raises a valid concern, be willing to adjust your proposal to address it. This shows you're open to compromise and ready to work together to find a solution.

That means when someone raises a valid objection, you must be willing to bend backward to address it. You must show that you're open to compromise and willing to work together to find a solution. So, get ready to stretch those negotiation muscles and start practicing your flexibility skills.

Follow Up with The Other Person

After addressing objections, following up with the other person is essential. This shows that you're committed to finding a solution that works for both parties and helps to build trust and rapport. When following up, address any concerns or objections the other person might have. This shows that you're taking their problems seriously and are willing to work together to find a solution.

Well, first of all, don't be like that guy who sends a follow-up email every day until he gets a response. Nobody likes that guy. Instead, be like the calm, confident person who understands that sometimes it takes time and patience to find a solution that works for everyone.

When you follow up, ensure you're addressing any remaining concerns or objections the other person might have. This shows that you're not just blindly pushing your agenda but are genuinely interested in finding a solution that works for both parties. And if you can inject a little bit of humor or personality into your follow-up message, all the better! Remember, it's all about building trust and rapport, not coming across as a desperate weirdo.

It's also important to be thorough when following up. If the other person is still hesitant, continue to address all their concerns and provide them with any additional information and evidence to support your proposal. Finally, to avoid objections in the future, it's vital to be proactive. Anticipate potential objections and address them before they become a problem.

The Art of Compromise: Finding a Win-Win Solution

Negotiation is a delicate art. It's like a dance, where each party takes a step forward and then a step back until they find the perfect rhythm. But what do you do when you reach an impasse? When it seems like neither party is willing to budge? That's when you need to master the art of compromise.

Compromise is all about finding a win-win solution. It's about finding a way for both parties to get what they want without sacrificing their values or needs. It's not about giving up or giving in but about finding a middle ground that works for everyone involved.

Identify Your Non-Negotiables

Before entering into a negotiation, it's essential to identify your non-negotiables. These are the things you absolutely cannot compromise on. Everything else is negotiable. Maybe it's your grandma's secret recipe for chili or your weird collection of antique spoons. Whatever it is, ensure you know your non-negotiables before heading into a negotiation.

Consider The Other Person's Perspective

Listening to the other party's perspective and understanding their needs and wants is essential. This can help you identify areas where compromise is possible. Please take a moment to hear the other person's perspective and get a feel for what they need. Then, figure out where you can meet in the middle. You give a little, and they provide a little. It's like negotiating with a toddler but with fewer tantrums (hopefully).

Be Clear with Your Proposal

Now, don't beat around the bush when you propose a compromise. Make sure you're clear about what you're offering and what you're asking for in return. This can prevent misunderstandings and ensure that both parties are on the same page. You don't want the other person to be like, "Wait, what did we agree to again?" That's just a recipe for disaster. So, spell it out. And if you're unsure, do what I do and draw a picture. A picture is worth a thousand words, and it's a lot harder to misinterpret.

Find Common Ground

Finding common ground is one of the best ways to reach a compromise. Look for things that you and your opponent have in common. It could be something as simple as a love for a particular sports team or a hobby. When you find common ground, it helps establish a connection.

When we talk about common ground, I don't mean that you both breathe oxygen or have two eyes (although those are great starting points, too). I'm talking about finding something you both genuinely enjoy or are passionate about. Maybe you both love watching the same sports team play. Or you both want knitted sweaters for your cats (don't worry, I won't judge you).

But let me tell you, finding common ground can lead to some hilarious situations. I once discovered that someone I had a little grudge against was also a huge fan of Nicolas Cage movies. Yes, you read that right, Nicolas Cage. We both couldn't stop talking about how much we loved "Con Air" and "National Treasure" (no shame here).

And you know what? Finding that common ground helped us see each other in a different light. We still didn't agree on everything, but we found some commonalities, which made a huge difference. So, don't be afraid to get a little weird when looking for common ground with your opponent. Who knows, you both may share a love for collecting antique spoons or making balloon animals.

Keep Your Emotions in Check

Negotiations can be emotional, but keeping your emotions in check is essential. Getting angry or defensive won't help you find a compromise. Instead, stay calm and level-headed, even if the other party is getting heated.

But here's the thing: losing your cool won't help you find a solution. So, keep those emotions in check, my friend. I know; it's easier said than done. It's like trying to stop binge-watching Netflix when you know you have a paper due tomorrow. But trust me, getting angry or defensive won't help.

Instead, stay calm and level-headed, take a deep breath, and count to ten. Or twenty. Or a hundred. Whatever it takes.

I can already hear some of you saying, "But what if the other party is getting heated?" Ah, yes, the classic "but what about them?" argument. Well, my friend, let me tell you a little secret. If you stay calm and collected, it's much harder for the other person to keep the rage train rolling.

So, there you have it, folks. The art of compromise in a nutshell. Identify your non-negotiables and consider the other person's perspective. Most importantly, be clear with your proposal and control your emotions. Stay calm and collected, and you'll be well on your way to finding a win-win solution.

Let me share a small secret before we go to the next stage. You see, most people make one crucial mistake in the world of negotiations: that's assuming the deal is done once both parties agree to the terms. But let me tell you, my friend, that's just the beginning of the journey.

The real battle begins when you have to put pen to paper and make it official. That's when things can get messy. That's when you realize the other party may not be as trustworthy as you thought. That's when you learn the importance of having a backup plan. In the next chapter, I will show you how to navigate this treacherous terrain and come out on top. Trust me; you don't want to miss it.

6

Chapter 6: The Fine Art of Closing

How to Seal the Deal

You've done the hard work. You've researched the other side's position, anticipated their objections, and found some common ground. Now, it's time to close the deal. Getting to yes can be daunting, but with the right approach, it doesn't have to be. Here are some tips to help you seal the deal and walk away a winner.

If you've ever found yourself on the verge of sealing the deal only to fumble and fall short, this chapter is for you. You will learn the psychology of closing and its various techniques. Also, you will learn closing tips and best practices and how to avoid mistakes when closing.

The Psychology of Closing

Closing a deal can be a daunting task for many people. Whether you're trying to sell a product or service, negotiate a salary, or get a date, closing requires a certain level of finesse and confidence. But what exactly goes into the psychology of closing? How can you seal the deal and achieve your desired outcome? Let's dive in and find out.

Firstly, it's essential to understand that closing is not just about convincing someone to do something they don't want to do. A successful close often involves tapping into a person's desires and needs and showing them how your proposition can fulfill them. Think of it as painting a picture in their mind, with your proposition as the solution to their problem.

As discussed in previous chapters, building rapport and establishing trust is another critical aspect of closing. People are likelier to say yes to someone they trust and feel comfortable around. This means listening to their needs, empathizing with their concerns, and addressing any objections.

However, it's also essential to be assertive and confident in your approach. If you come across as unsure or hesitant, you risk losing the other person's interest or confidence. This doesn't mean being aggressive or pushy but speaking with conviction and authority.

Common Mistakes People Make When Closing

Of course, not everyone will say yes to your proposition, no matter how well you present it. This is where the art of handling objections comes in. Rather than getting defensive or argumentative, try to understand the other person's concerns and address them respectfully and empathetically. Don't assume that a single approach will work for everyone. Each person is unique in their values, beliefs, and preferences. This means tailoring your approach to each individual and finding the right combination of strategies that will resonate with them.

Closing a deal is an art form that requires finesse, tact, and skill. But it's not just about mastering the art of persuasion; it's also about avoiding the common mistakes people make when trying to seal the deal. Here are some of the most common mistakes people make when closing and how you can prevent them.

Not Being Prepared

Preparation is critical to closing a deal. If you're not prepared, you'll come across as unprofessional and unorganized, making your client lose confidence in your ability to deliver. Sometimes, life gets in the way, and we forget to prepare for that crucial meeting or pitch. But if you walk into that room without any preparation, you might as well have just stepped in with your fly-down.

Your lack of preparation is like a spotlight on your incompetence, and your potential client will see right through it. They'll think, "This person can't even be bothered to prepare; how can I trust him or her to deliver on what they're promising?"

So, take some time to prepare. Do your research, know your pitch inside and out, and don't be caught with your pants down. Otherwise, you'll be left standing there feeling exposed and vulnerable, like in 6th grade when you showed up to school in your pajamas on what you thought was pajama day, and everyone laughed at you. Trust me; it's not a good feeling.

Not Listening to The Client

One of the most common mistakes people make when closing is not listening to their clients. They're so focused on making the sale that they forget to listen to their client's needs. Listening is critical to understanding your client's needs and concerns. You need to listen to be able to address their concerns and provide a solution that works for them.

Picture this: you're in a meeting trying to sell your product to a potential client. You've got your pitch down and ready to seal the deal. You start talking, and talking, and talking. You're so focused on conveying your message that you forget to listen to the client's needs. And then, suddenly, you realize you've been talking for so long that your client has fallen asleep. Yep, that's right, they're snoring right in front of you. Congratulations, you just lost the sale!

But don't worry; it's not all bad news. People often forget to listen to their clients and miss the mark completely. It's like trying to hit a target with a blindfold on - you'll miss it. So, remove that blindfold and listen to what your clients want. You might find that it's not what you thought it was. And who knows, you might even wake them up in the process.

The lesson here is simple: listen to your clients. Don't be so focused on making the sale that you forget their needs. Take the time to understand what they want, and then provide a solution that works for them. And if they do happen to fall asleep during your pitch, well, at least you'll know you tried.

Rushing The Sale

Another common mistake people make is rushing the sale. They're so eager to close the deal that they don't take the time to build rapport or establish trust with their client. Rushing the sale can make the client feel like they're being pushed into something uncomfortable, leading to them backing out of the deal altogether.

Let's say you've just met someone at a bar, and they seem pretty cool. You start a conversation, and within five minutes, you ask them if they want to marry you. Yeah, that's how ridiculous it can be to rush the sale.

Imagine you're trying to sell a product to someone, and you're so desperate to close the deal that you start throwing in free puppies and trips to the Bahamas. Okay, maybe that's an exaggeration, but you get the point.

Here's the thing: people need time to make a decision. They need to trust you and believe your offering will benefit them. So, take a step back, build rapport, and establish trust. And who knows, by the end, they'll be begging you to give them your product instead of the other way around.

Not Understanding the Client's Budget

Understanding your client's budget is essential to closing a deal. If you don't know what your client can afford. You may end up presenting them with options that are outside their budget, making them uncomfortable and leading them to walk away from the deal.

Imagine you're a car salesman, and you've finally convinced a client to take a look at the luxury car you've been trying to sell. You're feeling confident, have all your facts and figures ready to go, and are about to seal the deal. You show them the car and give them the rundown of all the fantastic features, and they love it. But then, you make a critical mistake. You forget to ask about their budget.

The client is excited about the car but hesitates when you tell them the price. They look at you, shocked, and you can practically see the money draining from their wallet. They can't afford the car price you just listed, and there is no more negotiating. This is a classic example of what not to do when closing a deal. Always, always, always know your client's budget.

It's like trying to sell caviar to someone who only eats mac and cheese. Sure, caviar is excellent, but it's not the right choice if they can't afford it. The same goes for closing a deal. Know your client's budget and present options that fit within their financial means. Trust me; it'll make the deal much smoother.

Focusing On the Wrong Features

When closing a deal, you must focus on the features that matter most to your client. If you're presenting them with features they don't care about, you're wasting their time and yours. While features are important, what matters to the other person is how your proposition can improve their life or solve their problem. So, instead of listing off features, focus on the benefits and outcomes they can expect.

Look, we all know that one person who just can't shut up about all their product or "amazing" features. They'll talk your ear off about all the bells and whistles, even though you're only interested in one thing. It's like trying to order a burger and having the waiter tell you about every ingredient in the kitchen.

Don't be that person. Nobody likes that person. You need to focus on the features that matter most to your client. If they're looking for a car with a kickass sound system, don't waste their time discussing the heated seats or the fancy GPS. Stick to what matters and close the damn deal already.

Not Addressing Objections

When trying to close a deal, you're likely to encounter objections. Ignoring these objections is a surefire way to lose the deal. Instead, it would help if you were prepared to address them head-on and provide solutions for your client's concerns.

Imagine trying to close a deal, and your client suddenly hits you with an objection. Maybe they're not sure if they can afford your product. Perhaps they're not convinced it will work for them. Maybe they're just having a bad day and want to give you a hard time. Whatever the case, you can't ignore their objection and hope it goes away. That's like trying to ignore a screaming baby on an airplane – it won't work.

Instead, you got to face that objection head-on, like a fearless gladiator in the Colosseum of sales. You have to devise a solution that addresses your client's concerns and shows them that you're not just trying to sell them snake oil. You could offer them a payment plan that fits their budget. You could show them some testimonials from happy customers in the same boat as them. You could pull out a magic wand and make all their problems disappear (okay, not that last one, but you get the point).

The bottom line is objections are going to happen. It's just a fact of life, like taxes and Mondays. But if you're prepared to handle them like a pro, you can turn those objections into opportunities and close that deal like a boss. And who doesn't want to be a boss?

Not Establishing a Timeline

Don't let the client determine the timeline of the sale. Be prepared and have a clear direction. If you're trying to close a deal and don't have a timeline, you might as well be playing a game of "let's see who blinks first" with your potential client. And let's be honest; nobody wants to play that game. It's like trying to cook a meal without a recipe or going on a road trip without a destination. You might end up somewhere, but it's probably not where you wanted to be. So, don't be that person who forgets to establish a timeline. Nobody likes that person. Setting a timeline is crucial to closing a deal. You risk losing the deal altogether if you don't have a clear timeline.

Not Knowing Your Competition

Knowing your competition is essential to closing a deal. If you don't know what your competition is offering. You won't be able to differentiate yourself and provide a compelling reason for your client to choose you over them.

Imagine you're a hot dog vendor trying to sell your hot dogs to hungry customers. But little do you know, there's a rival hot dog vendor across the street with a fancy neon sign and a celebrity endorsement. Without knowing what your competition offers, you're just another hot dog on the block, with nothing that makes you different. But if you know what your competition offers. You can devise a game plan to outsmart them, like providing free condiments or doing a taste test challenge. So don't be a blind hot dog vendor. Do your research and know your competition.

And trust me, you don't want to be caught off guard when your client says, "Well, your competition is offering X, Y, and Z. What do you have to offer?" And you're just standing there like a deer in headlights, with no comeback. That isn't very pleasant. So, do your due diligence and know your competition. Your wallet will thank you later.

Not Building Rapport

Building rapport with your client is essential to closing a deal. If you don't take the time to establish a connection with your client, they're less likely to trust you and less likely to do business with you. Trust me; nobody wants to do business with a robot that can't even crack a smile or crack a joke. Look them in the eyes and greet them with a firm handshake so they feel that they can trust you. This will also give you a chance to read your client's assuredness based on the handshake you get back.

But let me tell you, some people out there are just terrible at building rapport. They think they can waltz in and start spouting off their pitch without even introducing themselves or asking how the other person's day is going. It's like, dude, do you even want to close this deal? It will help if you put in a little effort to reap the rewards.

If you're struggling to build a connection with your client, try opening with a funny story or complimenting them on their choice of outfit. And for goodness sake, please put down your damn phone and pay attention to what they're saying. Building rapport takes time and effort, but it's ultimately worth it. Trust me; I'm not just saying that because I want you to buy my book. (Okay, maybe a little.)

Overpromising

Overpromising is a surefire way to lose a client's trust. If you promise more than you can deliver. Your client will likely feel disappointed and may even take their business elsewhere. Look, I get it. When you're closing a deal, you want to impress your client. You want to make them feel like they're getting the moon and the stars. But let me tell you, promising the moon and the stars is a surefire way to get your ass kicked.

When you promise more than you can deliver, your client will ask, "What the hell, man? You said we would get the moon and the stars, and now we're stuck with this lame-ass rock and some fireflies." And then they're going to be like, "You know what? We're taking our business elsewhere."

So don't be that person. Don't overpromise and underdeliver. If you're unsure you can deliver the moon and the stars, tell your client what you can do. Maybe it's not as flashy, but it's honest. And hey, honesty is the best policy.

Effective Strategies for Closing

Practical strategies for closing involve body language, confidence, timing, creating a sense of urgency, building rapport, and presenting a clear and compelling call to action. Using these strategies increases the likelihood of achieving your desired outcome and leaves a positive impression on those you communicate with.

Be Confident

If you don't believe in your proposition or yourself, it won't be easy to convince others to do so. This means preparing and rehearsing your pitch and practicing confidence-boosting techniques such as power poses and positive self-talk. Nobody will buy what you're selling if you can't convince yourself it's worth a damn.

That means practicing your pitch until you can recite it in your sleep and doing whatever it takes to pump yourself up beforehand. That could mean striking a power pose in the bathroom or giving yourself a little pep talk in the mirror. I've even heard of people listening to "Eye of the Tiger" on repeat to get themselves in the zone. Whatever works for you, do it.

But confidence isn't just about faking it till you make it. You got to believe in your product, too. I mean, believe in it. If you're selling a car, you had better know every spec and feature like the back of your hand. If you pitch a new software, you better have tested it out so much that you're practically a coder. And if you're trying to sell me on a kale smoothie, good luck with that. The point is the more you know and love what you're selling, the easier it is to close the deal.

Now, I know what you're thinking. "But, I'm not a naturally confident person. What am I supposed to do?" Well, I've got news for you, buttercup. Nobody is born a smooth-talking sales machine. It's all about practice and preparation. So, get out there and pitch to anyone who will listen: your grandma, your cat, or the cashier at the gas station. The more you do it, the better you'll get. And who knows? One day, you'll be closing deals like a boss, just like me.

Be Mindful of Your Body Language

Pay close attention to your customer's body language and vocal cues. Are they nodding along and asking questions, or are they looking at their watch and trying to end the conversation? The former is a good sign that they're ready to close, while the latter is a sign that you need to adjust your approach. Please pay attention to their body language, facial expressions, and tone of voice, as these can provide important clues about their level of interest, engagement, and commitment.

Be mindful of their eye movement. Typically, if a person glances up to their left, that means the person is supposedly telling the truth. A glance to the upper right may mean they recall a memory or lie. Looking down to their left may mean they are assessing their feelings. While looking down to the right could indicate that an internal dialog is going on.

For example, if your prospect seems distracted, uninterested, or skeptical, postpone the closing until you can address their concerns and build more rapport. On the other hand, if your prospect is nodding along, asking questions, and showing enthusiasm, it may be an excellent time to push for a commitment.

Create A Sense of Urgency or Scarcity

This can be done by highlighting the benefits of your offer, emphasizing any time-sensitive incentives or discounts, or even mentioning that other buyers are interested in the same opportunity. However, be careful not to overuse these tactics or come across as manipulative or pushy. Your goal should be to inspire your prospects to take action based on their desires and motivations rather than pressuring them into a decision they may regret later.

People are more likely to take action when they feel like they may miss out on something valuable. This could involve offering a limited-time discount, highlighting the scarcity of your product or service, or creating a sense of FOMO (fear of missing out).

First, don't just tell them how great your product is; make them feel it in their bones. You want them to say, "Damn, I need this in my life." And if that doesn't work, you can always resort to the classic, "Other buyers are interested in this too, you know." That'll get them sweating.

Next, time is of the essence. People love feeling like they're getting a good deal, but they love it even more when they know that deal won't last forever. So, make sure to mention any time-sensitive incentives or discounts. It's like when you were about to buy those concert tickets, and the website said, "Only 2 left!" Suddenly, you didn't care about the price anymore; you just needed those tickets.

Now, I know what you're thinking. "But won't that make me seem manipulative and pushy?" Well, yeah, it could. That's why you've got to balance it out with some positive vibes. Ensure to inspire your prospects to take action based on their desires and motivations. After all, you don't want them to feel like they got swindled into something they didn't like. That's a surefire way to get some bad reviews on Yelp.

Use Silence to Your Advantage

Silence can be uncomfortable, but it's also a powerful negotiating tool. Don't be afraid to let the other side speak first when negotiating. They may reveal information that can help you make a stronger case.

Let me give you an example. Once, I was negotiating with this dude trying to sell me a used car. He was going on and on about all the fancy and how great the car was. And you know what I did? I just shut my trap and let him talk.

And you know what happened? He started revealing all sorts of information. He told me about how the car had been in a few accidents and how he was desperate to sell it because he needed the money to pay off his gambling debts. I mean, talk about oversharing!

Thanks to my effective use of silence, I negotiated a killer deal on that car. And all I had to do was sit there and look interested. So, my friend, remember the power of silence the next time you're negotiating. Don't be afraid to let the other person talk first. Who knows what juicy tidbits they'll reveal? So remember, when in doubt, just shut your trap and let the other person do the talking.

Timing: Knowing When to Close

Timing is everything, and we'll show you how to recognize the perfect moment to strike. If you wait too long, the other person may lose interest or become distracted. On the other hand, if you act too soon, you may come across as pushy or desperate. It's about finding the right moment and reading the other person's cues.

Knowing when to close is crucial to sealing the deal and to avoid losing it altogether. Timing is everything, and nowhere is that more accurate than in sales. You can have the best product or idea, the most persuasive pitch, and the perfect customer, but you'll be left with nothing if you don't time your close right.

The best time to close is when your opponent is ready to buy into your idea or product. This may seem obvious, but many people (mainly salespeople) miss this critical moment because they're too eager to close or afraid to ask for the sale. In sales, closing too early can turn off potential customers who feel pressured or rushed. On the other hand, waiting too long can allow your competition to swoop in and steal the deal.

Timing also plays a role in the type of close you use. For example, a direct close may be appropriate if the other person is ready to buy into your idea or product. While an indirect close may be more effective if they need more time to think.

Be Willing to Walk Away

This might seem counterintuitive, but sometimes, the best way to get what you want is to be willing to walk away. If the other side isn't ready to meet your needs, be prepared to walk away and find another solution.

Let me give you an example. Imagine you're at a pet store, trying to buy a goldfish. You want a big one with those fancy scales that shimmer in the light. But the store only has tiny, boring fish that look like they belong in a fishbowl at a dentist's office.

Now, you could settle for one of those little guys. You could convince yourself that size doesn't matter and that a tiny fish will still make a great addition to your living room. But no, my friend, that's not how you get what you want. Instead, you've got to be willing to walk away. You got to put on your best "I don't need this shit" face and head for the door. And when you're about to leave, the pet store owner will call out to you. "Wait! I have something in the back! Something special!"

And you'll turn around because you're curious. And the pet store owner will come out with a giant, shimmering goldfish twice the size of the tiny ones in the tank. And you'll know, at that moment, that you made the right decision by walking away. So, my friend, remember this - sometimes, you must be willing to walk away. You have to show the other side that you're not desperate and will not settle for less than what you want. And who knows, they just may surprise you with something even better than you initially requested.

Follow Up After Closing

Once you've successfully closed the deal, following up and ensuring everything is on track is essential. This could include sending a thank-you note or email, checking progress, and addressing any concerns or issues. By maintaining open lines of communication, you can help ensure a positive outcome and set the stage for future business opportunities.

Celebrate Your Success

You've done the hard work and negotiated like a boss, and now it's time to celebrate like there's no tomorrow. Go ahead, pop that champagne, throw your hands in the air, and let out a victory yell that would make even the most stoic negotiators proud.

Negotiating is like convincing your parents to let you have a party while they're out of town. It's a delicate balance of persuasion, charm, and some bullshit thrown in for good measure. And when you finally get the green light, you feel like you just won the lottery.

So, take a moment to bask in your success. You deserve it because you're magnificent. Whether you negotiated a raise, a better deal on a car, or just convinced your partner to try that new restaurant you've been eyeing, you did it. And that's something to be proud of.

And let's be honest; celebrating your success is the best part of negotiating. It's like getting a participation trophy but earning it. So go ahead, treat yourself. Buy that fancy bottle of wine, indulge in a fancy dinner, or take a weekend getaway. Whatever makes you feel like a baller, please do it.

Closing the deal can be the most challenging part of the negotiation process, but you can walk away a winner with these tips. Remain confident and be willing to make concessions when necessary. And above all, remember that negotiation is a skill that can be learned and improved over time. So, keep practicing, learning, and getting what you want.

7

Chapter 7: Putting it All Together

Welcome to the final chapter of "Bye-Bye Bluffer"! If you've made it this far, congratulations! You're well on your way to becoming a master of reading people's body language and winning them over. But don't get too comfortable just yet - we're about to take things to the next level.

In this chapter, we will talk about how to put all of your new-found skills together to become a force to be reckoned with. We'll cover everything from practicing and refining your abilities to finding opportunities to put them into action and staying ahead with continuous learning.

Next, we'll talk about how to find opportunities to practice your skills. After all, what good are your skills if you never have a chance to use them? We'll share some strategies for building your network and connections and getting your foot in the door.

But it's not just about practicing - you need to put your skills to the test in the real world. We'll dive into how to take action and apply your abilities to real-life situations. This is where the rubber meets the road and where you'll start to see the fruits of your labor. You'll be a lean, mean, skill-having machine by the time you're done. Let's get started!

Practicing and Refining Your Skills: Tips and Techniques for Improving Your Abilities

Let's start with the basics: practice. It may seem obvious, but it's the only way to get better at reading people's body language and winning them over. You can read all the books, watch all the tutorials, and take all the classes you want, but if you don't practice, you won't improve. When I say practice, I don't mean just going through the motions. It would help if you practiced with intention. That means setting specific goals for yourself and focusing on the areas where you need improvement. It also means pushing yourself out of your comfort zone and trying new things.

Take your newly honed skills on the road. Try negotiating and reading body language with all different types of people. So head down to a used car lot, thrift store, or street vendor and spark a conversation. Put those new negotiating skills to the test.

Focus On the Process, Not Just the Outcome

It's easy to get caught up in the result and forget about the work that goes into getting there. But the process is where the real growth happens. Focus on every application of the steps of reading body language and winning people over your product or idea.

It's not just about the end goal of getting someone to buy into your idea or product. It's about the journey, my friend. Observing and understanding body language can be just as rewarding as a result. Have you ever tried to read someone's body language and missed the mark? It happens to the best of us. But that's where the real growth happens. You can learn from your mistakes and get better with practice.

And let me tell you, there's nothing more satisfying than nailing that perfect pitch and seeing the other person's body language shift in your favor. It's like a high-five from the universe. So remember to enjoy the process, my friend, and observe those nonverbal cues like the boss you are.

Stay Motivated

This can be tough, especially when progress is slow, or you hit a plateau. But staying motivated is essential if you want to continue improving. Find ways to stay inspired, whether by connecting with others in this area of expertise or reading inspirational stories of the most remarkable salespeople.

I know reading people's body language can be tricky. It's like trying to decipher a secret code that only they know. But if you want to win them over, you must stay motivated. Now, I'm not saying you should read some boring textbook on body language. No way. Instead, try connecting with people who are just as lost as you are. You could form a support group. You can call it "Confused About Body Language Anonymous." Or "CABLA" for short.

And if that doesn't work, read some inspirational stories of the most excellent salespeople out there. Maybe you'll find comfort in the fact that they, too, had to figure out what a raised eyebrow means. So, stay motivated, my friend. You got this.

Experiment and use Visualization

Don't be afraid to try new things and take risks. This can help you discover new approaches or techniques for reading people's body language and winning them over. It can also help you break out of any ruts you may be in and keep things fresh and exciting. You can't fear stepping out of your comfort zone and trying something new. That could mean doing a little dance while you pitch your idea or wearing a funny hat to your next meeting. Who knows? The point is you got to be willing to take a chance.

And once you've got the confidence to try new things, you can start using the power of Visualization. That's right; I said Visualization. You got to picture yourself succeeding before it even happens. Imagine reading people's body language like a pro and winning them with charm and wit. See yourself doing the moonwalk while your client signs the contract. Whatever works for you, man. Just make sure you see it in your mind's eye. So, take risks, visualize your success, and don't fear getting weird. Before you know it, you'll read people's body language like a pro and close deals left and right.

Break Down Your Practice Sessions

Breaking down your practice sessions into smaller, manageable skills can prove to be effective. This can help you avoid feeling overwhelmed and make seeing progress easier. Set achievable goals for each practice session and focus on one skill at a time. Don't try to master everything at once. Focus on one skill at a time and give yourself time to rest and recharge.

Take a break and watch some funny cat videos. One thing that many people overlook when practicing their skills is the importance of rest. It's tempting to work non-stop when trying to improve, but taking breaks and giving yourself time to rest is essential for long-term progress.

But don't get too comfortable on that break. Keep in mind that the best way to improve is through repetition. So, don't be afraid to practice on unsuspecting strangers in public places. Just don't get arrested for being a creepy weirdo.

Overcome Fear

Have you ever tried to read someone's body language and felt like a complete failure? Maybe you misread a smirk as a smile or mistook a frown for confusion. It happens to the best of us. But here's the thing: you can't let the fear of getting it wrong hold you back. You might make a few mistakes, but that's how you learn and improve. So, instead of being afraid of misreading body language, use it as a motivator to keep practicing and honing your skills.

And let's be honest, sometimes people's body language is just downright confusing. They might be nodding but having a scowl or crossing their arms but smiling simultaneously. They're playing some twisted game of "Guess what I'm feeling." But don't let that discourage you. Keep observing and analyzing their body language; if all else fails, ask them how they're feeling. You might be surprised at how much easier it is to communicate when you ask.

Remember, fear is a natural part of the learning process. Feeling a little scared or uncertain when trying to improve your skills is okay, but don't let it hold you back. Embrace the fear and use it as motivation to keep pushing forward. And hey, even if you misread someone's body language, you can laugh about it later.

Embrace Failure and Learn from Others

Nobody is perfect, and everyone makes mistakes. Instead of getting discouraged when you fail at convincing someone, use it as an opportunity to learn. Analyze what went wrong, determine what you can do differently next time, and keep moving forward. You might read someone's crossed arms as a sign of disinterest when they have an itch on their shoulder. Or maybe you'll mistake someone's nervous fidgeting for boredom when they just have an upset stomach. It happens to the best of us.

But don't let those failures get you down. Instead, use them as a chance to learn and improve. Next time, you'll pick up on the subtle eyebrow raise that indicates interest or how someone leans forward when excited about a topic. And if you're committed to mastering the art of body language, seek mentors or experts who can teach you even more tricks of the trade.

But most importantly, remember that no matter how much you learn, you'll never be 100% right all the time. People are complicated creatures and sometimes don't even know what their body language means. Seek out mentors or other experts in the field and learn from them. Read other books or articles by people skilled in this area of interest. Attend workshops or seminars where you can learn from experts. The more you can learn from others, the faster you'll be able to improve.

Seek Out Feedback

Hearing criticism sucks. It's like getting hit in the face with a sack of potatoes. But hey, if you want to improve your persuasion skills, you must suck it up and ask for feedback. Find someone who knows their stuff and ask them to give you constructive criticism. Don't ask your mom; she'll tell you you're perfect. If you can't find anyone to provide feedback, evaluate yourself. Take a good, hard look in the mirror and ask yourself, "Am I coming across as a sleazy salesman or a genuine human being?" Be honest with yourself, even if it hurts a little.

Now, I know what you're thinking. "But I don't want to hear all the bad things I'm doing wrong!" Well, tough cookies, buttercup. You got to take the good with the bad. The more you know about your weaknesses, the better you can improve. So, chin up and take those feedback punches like a champ!

Celebrate Your Progress

Look, we all know how it feels to be stuck in a cycle of constant self-improvement. We're always looking for ways to get better, be more persuasive, and win more people over. But you know what's important too? When you take a damn break every once in a while and pat yourself on the back.

Did you close a deal? Congratulations! You got someone to say "yes" to your proposition? That's awesome! Take a moment to celebrate your success, no matter how small. Dance around your office like a crazy person, treat yourself to a fancy coffee, or give yourself a well-deserved high-five. You deserve it.

Remember, the road to success isn't just about constantly improving yourself. It's also about taking time to appreciate the progress you've already made and using that as motivation to keep going. So, the next time you close a deal, don't just move on to the next one without celebrating. Take a moment to revel in your victory, and then return to work.

Building Networks, Connections, And Exposure

As I previously stated, you can't become a master overnight. You need to practice, practice, practice! And one of the best ways to do that is by building your network and connections. But wait, before you start panicking and thinking, "I don't have a network!" take a deep breath and relax. Building a network doesn't mean you need to have a thousand Facebook friends or LinkedIn connections. It means you need to start expanding your social circle.

Build Networks

One great way to do that is by attending events related to your interests or industry. Whether it's a conference, seminar, or networking event, it's an excellent opportunity to meet new people and learn from experts in your field. Plus, you'll be surrounded by like-minded individuals who share your passions.

But attending events isn't just about handing out business cards and hoping for the best. You need to be strategic in your approach. Start by doing some research on the event and its attendees. Who will be there? What are their interests and backgrounds? This will give you a better idea of who you want to connect with and how you can add value to their lives.

Of course, building your network isn't just about finding opportunities to practice your people skills. It's also about creating opportunities for yourself. The more people you know, the more chances you'll have to learn, grow, and advance in your career. But, as with anything in life, there's a catch. You can't just build a network and expect things to happen magically. You need to be proactive and seek out opportunities. This means keeping an eye out for job postings, asking for referrals, and being open to new experiences.

Staying Informed and Up-To-Date

In addition to building your network, staying informed and up-to-date on industry trends and news is essential. This will help you converse with others and position you as a thought leader and expert in your field. One way to stay informed is by reading blogs, newsletters, and industry publications. But don't just read passively. Engage with the content and share your thoughts and opinions. This will help you build your brand and establish yourself as a valuable asset in your industry.

Making Meaningful Connections

Building your network isn't just about professional connections. It's also about making meaningful connections with the people in your personal life. This means investing time and energy into your friendships and relationships. But, just like with professional networking, it's essential to be strategic in your approach. Start by identifying the most important people to you and finding ways to stay connected. The honesty and integrity you show toward your friendships may give confidence in them, which can lead to future business referrals for yourself in the future. This might mean scheduling regular catch-ups or finding shared activities to do together.

It's also important to be present and engaged when spending time with the people in your personal life. Put away your phone, listen actively, and show a genuine interest in what they say. This will help you build more profound and meaningful relationships. And, just like with professional networking, staying in touch and showing that you value your relationships is crucial. Send a text message or make a phone call to check in and see how someone is doing. Small gestures can go a long way in maintaining strong and healthy relationships.

Traveling And Experiencing New Cultures

This can be a great way to expand your worldview and learn more about the people around you. It can also be an excellent opportunity to practice your communication skills in a new and challenging environment. But when traveling, respecting the local culture and customs is essential. Do your research before you go, and be willing to adapt and learn. And, most importantly, be open to new experiences and ways of thinking.

Of course, building your network isn't just about finding opportunities to practice your people skills. It's also about finding ways to add value to the lives of others. This means being willing to help and support others, even when there's nothing in it for you.

Mentoring Or Coaching

Whether in your professional or personal life, mentoring can be a great way to share your knowledge and experience with others while also learning and growing yourself. But, just like with networking, it's essential to be strategic in your approach to mentoring. Find people who are genuinely committed to learning and growing and who are willing to put in the work. And, most importantly, be patient and understanding. Mentoring takes time and effort, but the rewards can be truly life-changing.

Volunteering

Whether volunteering at a local charity or organization or simply helping out a friend or family member in need, volunteering can be a great way to give back and make a difference. But, as with mentoring, it's essential to be strategic in your approach to volunteering. Find causes or organizations that align with your values and passions, and find ways to make a real impact. And, most importantly, be consistent and committed. Volunteering takes time and effort, but the rewards are immeasurable.

Building your network and connections is a great way to practice your people skills and create opportunities for yourself. Whether it's through attending events, volunteering, or mentoring, there are countless ways to expand your social circle and make meaningful connections. But, as with anything, it takes time, effort, and a willingness to learn and grow. So, go out there, be strategic, be patient, and most importantly, have fun!

Conclusion

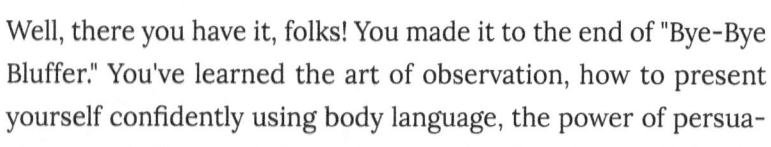

Well, there you have it, folks! You made it to the end of "Bye-Bye Bluffer." You've learned the art of observation, how to present yourself confidently using body language, the power of persuasive speech, the psychology of persuasion, how to negotiate, the fine art of closing, and how to bring all these skills together to take you to the next level.

It's difficult to read people, but now you are armed with the tools to do just that. You know how to present yourself confidently, use language to win people over, and negotiate to get what you want. You've learned how to close deals and combine all these skills to be your best version.

But most importantly, you will now stay focused and be accurate. You've learned to read between the lines and see the truth behind the words and actions. Be authentic and honest, even when it's complicated. And that, my friends, sets you apart from the bluffers. So go forth and conquer the world. Use your newfound skills to win people over and get what you want. But remember to keep it real along the way. After all, there's no point in winning if you're not being your true self.

Good luck, and remember: bye-bye bluffer, hello authentic self!

Acknowledgments

First, I would like to thank my incredible husband, who gave me great feedback during the writing process. I have walked many paths to be where I am now, and you have been my rock through it all. Thank you for lighting the fire under my ass when I feel like sometimes giving up. All my mentors in sales that have taught me most of the information in this book. You taught me some tricks that helped me make some big commission checks. Thank you to my parents for bringing me into this crazy world and for believing in me no matter what. I love you so much, and thank you for putting up with my crap. To my bandmates, who always encourage me to keep on going even when I get frustrated with writer's block. Thank you to my editor for tightening up my sloppy messes. I couldn't have done this without you. Although it's taken longer than I would have liked to pursue my dream of being an Author, I'm glad to say I have finally published my first book! Believe me, I'm celebrating in my largest "Power Pose"!

Most importantly, thank you to everyone who decided to read this straightforward, witty sales book of mine. I hope, at some point, it made you think, laugh, or, at the very least, entertain you. Without my supporters, none of this would be possible. So, thank you for believing in me and helping this book be as successful as it is!

Unlock the Power of Generosity

Now that you've mastered the art of body language and bluffer-busting, it's time to pass that knowledge forward.

Here's how you can make a difference: **Leave a review.**

Your review could help...

- one more person master the art of observation.

- one more professional ace their negotiations.

- one more individual stop getting bluffed and start seeing the truth.

Thank you from the bottom of my heart. Now, back to mastering the power of body language!

— Your biggest fan, A.M. Corby

Leave a review here:

About The Author

A.M. Corby was born in southern California and raised in California, Ohio, and Hawaii. She became a master certified automotive and diesel mechanic with Ohio Auto Diesel Tech College. This led her into the automotive industry, practicing everything from Mechanic, Service Advisor, Parts, Sales and Management.

Her experience as a telemarketer at the age of 14 was just the experience she needed to set her apart from the rest. Just like most driven young salespeople, Corby has enjoyed receiving her many promotions in various fields. She has continued to have a career in the area of Sales and Management for over 25 years.

Corby is fortunate to have learned from the best, from CEOs to investment bankers, top salesmen, and politicians. Her first full-length book explores the art of observation, the power of body language, and how to present yourself confidently. Using her long experience in the sales industry, she teaches the reader the psychology of persuasion and negotiation, giving them the tools to acquire what they want in life and to "seal the deal" like a boss.

Her obsession with acquiring knowledge led her to pursue licensing as a Realtor and a Mortgage Loan Officer, as well as her intricate studies in Floral Design school. Besides her passion for sales, fast cars, and loud music, she has always had a love for books and began writing poetry at the age of 8. Now, she converts her poems into song lyrics that she still performs live. In her free time, she enjoys an eclectic range of interests, including reading, writing music, singing, and playing guitar. She also enjoys curling, anything involving the outdoors, and her involvement with the Irish dancing community.

Today, Corby enjoys living in Las Vegas, Nevada, with her husband. As far as her future is concerned, Corby is passionate about helping others succeed in life. She continues her travels, exploring new places, and documenting her experiences to share them with as many people as she possibly can.

You can contact and connect with A.M. Corby at amcorby.com

www.ingramcontent.com/pod-product-compliance
Lightning Source LLC
Chambersburg PA
CBHW020412130626
46549CB00006B/2532